The Word

1969–70
1970–71

Writings by the Author

The Ultimate
Success Is Normal, Just Be Yourself,
   Your Eternal Identity
Fulfillment of Purpose, Volume One
Fulfillment of Purpose, Volume Two
You Are the Splendor
Gems & Poems of The Ultimate
The Gospel According to Thomas
Three Essential Steps
The Omnipresent I Am, Volume One
The Omnipresent I Am, Evidenced, Volume Two
The Ultimate Awareness, an Eternal Constant,
   Volume One
The Ultimate Awareness, an Eternal Constant,
   Volume Two
The Word 1960-1973
   (9-Volume Series)
Questions & Answers from The Word

These and other books available through:

Mystics of the World
Eliot, Maine
www.mysticsoftheworld.com

The Word

1969–70
1970–71

Marie S. Watts

The Word

1969–70

1970–71

by Marie S. Watts

Mystics of the World First Edition 2016
Published by Mystics of the World
ISBN-13:978-1-946362-04-9
ISBN-10:1-946362-04-2

For information contact:

Mystics of the World
Eliot, Maine
www.mysticsoftheworld.com

Cover Graphics by Margra Muirhead
Printed by CreateSpace
Available from:

      Mystics of the World.com
      Amazon.com

Contents

Note to the Reader

The Word first appeared as monthly letters sent by Marie Watts to students of the Ultimate, beginning with March and ending with February of the following year. She was at first reluctant to begin this publication, even though she sensed that it had to be done. She explains her resistance in the letter of February 1964:

> As you know, I have never wanted any personal element to enter into the activity of the Ultimate. Above all, I did not want a monthly publication to be a personal message from an assumptive leader to followers who believed that they were limited. However, one evening the title for this activity was clearly revealed; this title was so impersonal that all my reluctance dissolved, and *The Word* has been an impersonal monthly message of Truth.

Marie traveled throughout the country, giving classes and lectures. She lived constantly in a state of divine inspiration, and everything she shared flowed forth from this enlightened Consciousness. She shared these divine unfoldments in *The Word* and in her books, enabling students of the Ultimate to develop deeper understanding in specific areas and thereby rise higher in Consciousness, ultimately reaching a state of enlightenment.

From the beginning, the response from readers was one of tremendous gratitude and love. Letters came almost daily, reporting great revelation, inspiration, and so-called healing through the study and contemplation of *The Word*. She gives two reasons for this:

Daily and nightly revelations continue increasingly in the Consciousness of the *I* that I am. But it is also true that this same revelation continues to take place increasingly as the Consciousness of the I AM that you are. ... The revelations appearing in *The Word* are no more my revelations than they are *your* revelations (*The Word*, March 1962).

One reader was moved to write "A Tribute to *The Word*," which Marie included in the 1963 November issue. It reads in part:

When *The Word* is read for the first time, there is a feeling of fullness; then, as it is reread again and again, there is no longer a reason to read anymore, but just let the Light that I am *be* the Self that I am .... Be patient in your contemplations, and *The Word* will do the rest. It is a Pearl of great price. No price can be put upon it, for its value can only be revealed as you contemplate the Truth it states. *The Word* is You, *God identified*, the Christ.

Marie often expressed her great joy in witnessing the divine fulfillment of *The Word*. The deep spiritual Truth contained in these writings is indeed timeless and will be of untold value to any sincere spiritual seeker.

We are aware that our Consciousness is boundless. We are also aware that the Consciousness of everyone is boundless. Thus, we know that anyone who is ready to perceive any specific Truth we are knowing may also perceive this same Truth.

This is unselfed Love in action. This is the way in which the world must be enlightened. Above all, this is the way it is taking place. It is a glorious experience to realize that every silent contemplation is going on not only as the Consciousness of the

Identity who is contemplating, but also as the world Consciousness. It has to be this way because the Consciousness of the Identity is the world Consciousness and the Universal Consciousness (*The Word*, Dec. 1963).

The Word

1969–70

March 1969

*In the beginning was the Word, and the Word was
with God, and the Word was God.*

—*John 1:1*

Dear One,

I must thank you for your many letters expressing joy
in the glowing experiences realized through the study of
the first volume of our most recent classnotes [*The Ultimate
Awareness, an Eternal Constant, Vol. 1*]. Some of you have
reported that your first experience in full illumination was
realized during your study of this book. Some have told,
with joy, of so-called healing. Needless to say, my Heart
literally sings with joy.

Let us consider the world as it appears to be today.
True it is, the appearance is disturbing, and there seems to
be much gloom and discouragement. But even the world
of appearance is not all bad. It is indeed inspiring to consider how the mistakenly accepted so-called limitations
are being obliterated. And of course, many of us are not
surprised that it is possible to be free of the Earth planet's
confinement. Greater than all is the fact that Man, the
Christ, was never confined, nor can he be limited in anyway. But it is well to contemplate including this world in
Consciousness quite frequently. It is a joy to know that
our seeing is being realized everywhere and that the
Power of this contemplation is not limited or confined
anywhere. This, Beloved, is our way of helping the world.
Beyond and behind any apparent discord, there is always
Absolute Perfection. Thus, strictly speaking, no "help" is
needed. Yet we perceive the necessity of consciously
seeing the world as it is. Thus, we love, and we act lovingly.

Being Versus Doing

Most of us who have now arrived at the Absolute have come through many paths. Almost always our paths have been concerned with metaphysics. Well, we know the Absolute is not metaphysics. Metaphysics deals primarily with so-called cause and effect, God and man, etc. We are grateful for every path we have followed on our way; however, there is one aspect of our metaphysical study that seems to remain stubbornly with us, and this is the practice of doing "mental work." Sometimes we will be so sure we have "seen through" this aspect of duality, only to find that inadvertently we are again trying to do something about some seeming problem. This is seemingly a stumbling block for many of us. Then, paradoxically, the question would arise: "But what can I *do* about it?" (If it weren't so serious, it would be amusing.)

Well, there is a way, but this way has nothing to do with mental work or trying to do right thinking, etc. The way is infinite Awareness of Being. Jesus knew—and knows—this way. But Beloved, you also know the way. When Jesus said, "Whither I go ye know, and the way ye know," he was speaking with the disciples. He plainly stated that the disciples knew the way, even as Jesus, you, I, everyone, really knows the way. Jesus knew that the disciples could not be alive, could not be conscious, unless they knew, or were inherently aware of being, *Infinite Consciousness.*

There is no such thing as Infinitude *and* you. Neither can there be you *and* Infinite. The seeming difficulty stems from the basic fallacy that we can exist as anyone or anything that is not Infinity. *There is only Infinite Consciousness that is conscious at all. Therefore, there is only Infinite Consciousness aware of Being.* Unless we clearly perceive that it is Infinite Consciousness that is aware of being right here, we are going to seem to stumble over the block of duality. You see, it is this supposed separate you, with a separate consciousness of your own, that appears to have or to be conscious of all the problems.

Infinite Consciousness, or Awareness of Being, is infinitely, omnipresently conscious, *aware of Being*. This Consciousness can have no awareness of Being other than as *just what this Consciousness is*. And of course, all of this is God aware of being God. Naturally then, Infinite Consciousness is never aware of problems that have to be worked out or of any mental gymnastics in order to change something that is already constantly, eternally perfect. Now always we are alert to the fact that it is this Infinite Consciousness that is aware of being right here, right now.

This Infinite Consciousness knows nothing of a world or worlds in strife, trouble, or at war. It knows nothing of any of the so-called material laws that are supposed to govern man and nation. It knows nothing of so-called medical laws or of any laws pertaining to a supposedly born man. You ask, "What has this to do with the Body?" Beloved, the very Substance that is consciously, eternally alive right here and now is Infinite *Awareness of Being*. Does this mean that you are not an Identity? Not at all. It means that *this Identity right here is Infinity iden-tified*, and this Body right here and now is Infinity, or Infinite Awareness of being, *being* this Body.

Now you can see why it is so necessary to perceive clearly the Infinite Nature of everything and everyone. It is essential to perceive the Infinite Nature of *all* Substance in Form. But this is not all. We must perceive that it is Infinity that is acting, moving, being, right here, as the *only* activity that is ever going on.

That which follows is not something to go over and over in the hope that it will reveal some method or for-mula for the solution of something called a problem. It is just something that has to be written right here and now. I do know that these Truths will reveal the futility of any attempt to practice mentally or do something about some so-called problem.

Now, Beloved, because every Identity is the one *I* identified, each can speak these Truths in his own words, as himself:

It is infinite Life that is alive here, and not a little temporary born life. I am alive; thus, I am infinite, eternal Life *living* right here. It is infinite, eternal Consciousness that is conscious here, and not a confined, temporary, limited, born consciousness. I am conscious; thus, I am this infinite, eternal Consciousness, being conscious right here.

It is infinite, unlimited Intelligence, Mind, that *knows* and is all complete knowledge here, and not a limited little separate mind confined to a born brain. *I know*; thus, it is infinite, eternal, all-knowing Intelligence being intelligent right here.

Oh, joyous Ecstasy, it is Infinity being infinite right here, right now, and *I am That*. These Truths being revealed are simple statements of Absolute Facts. *They are the Word Itself, and I am That.*

It is infinite Love that loves here—boundless, impersonal, complete—and not a little separate, personal love that merely loves certain supposed "other" ones. I Love; thus, I am infinite, eternal, constant Love, loving right here and now. It is infinite, absolute, eternal, constant Perfection that is perfect now, and not a little separate perfection confined in a supposed born body. I am infinite Perfection being perfect right here.

It is infinite, immutable, eternal Substance, *Awareness of Being*, that is in Form here, and not a temporary, born, mutable substance in a temporary form. I am aware *of* this Body; thus, I am aware of *being* this Body. Therefore, I am Infinity in Form right here and now. It is infinite Identity identified here, and not a so-called temporary born identity.

It is infinite Vision that sees here, and not a finite, limited, separate vision. *I see*. I see all as it is. I am

16

conscious *of* vision. I am conscious *as* Vision. The
Vision that is seeing right here and now is the infinite
Vision seeing.

It is infinite Completeness that is complete here,
and not merely a little separate temporary wholeness
enclosed in a supposedly born body. I am complete;
thus, I am infinitely complete. I am infinite Completeness, Wholeness, being complete right here and now.

It is infinite, intelligent, principled, perfect Government that governs here, and not a separate, temporary,
self-governed supposed born body. I am aware of this
infinite Government; thus, I am conscious *as* this Government. I am infinite, perfect, immutable Government,
governing right here and now. Yes, the infinite, eternal
I that I am *is* the eternal Body that I am. Therefore, I
am the infinite, boundless Body, being this Body right
here and now.

Beloved, it is now clear there should be no mental
work involved in this way of "seeing." Do not try to
interpret the foregoing statements. It would be futile.
Above all, realize that it would be futile to consider them
as affirmations and denials. As you read, just let these
Absolute Truths reveal themselves in ever greater glory.
You see, these Truths are already present in and as the
infinite Awareness of Being that you are. Let them just
continue to surge and flow as the infinite Consciousness
you are. Paul stated it very clearly when he said, "Let this
mind be in you, which was also in Christ Jesus." Well, it
already is the Consciousness you are. Just let it *be*.

When Jesus spoke these wonderful words, "I am the
way," he was not speaking for himself alone. Neither was
he speaking only for the disciples or those who were
hearing him. Rather, he was speaking for you, for everyone.
But even more important is the fact that he was speaking
as the Consciousness that you are, that I am, that is conscious as everyone. There really is one infinite, indivisible

Consciousness, and our awareness of being this *one* Consciousness is the way.

Beloved, for so long it *seemed* that we were seeking the way; how wonderful it is to realize that all the while *we were the Way* we apparently sought. Now we all can say, "I am the Way, the Truth, and the Life." For it is in being the Way that we have discovered our boundless, infinite Self. Thus it is that we know, and we know that we know.

Light and Love,
Marie S. Watts

April 1969

In the beginning was the Word, and the Word was
with God, and the Word was God.

—John 1:1

Dear One,

I must thank you for your many letters expressing such Joy in the inspiration and Light you experience. Needless to say, as you rejoice, so it is that we also rejoice.

Some of you have questioned our frequent use of the word *God*. Generally, an objection to the word stems from an orthodox experience or background, in which God was supposed to be a man-like deity and completely separated from the Identity. There are some sincere students who find that the word *God* has a tendency to make them feel as though they were separate from the infinite Allness which *is* God. Of course, no word or combination of words can possibly express the *feeling* that is engendered through the Consciousness of God *being* the Entirety of our Existence and the Entirety of All Existence. But words can only fulfill their purpose according to what these words mean to the Identity. No word has meaning *for* you unless it has meaning *to* you.

In my experience, the word *God* is of the utmost importance. It has an inexpressible depth of meaning that goes beyond all other words in the vocabulary. In my Awareness, the word *God* is always synonymous with the word *Love*. When I am speaking the word *God*, I am aware that I am also speaking the word *Love*. There is always a wonderful sense of warmth and tenderness that surges and flows when I speak or write the word *God*.

But this is not all. To me, this wonderful word means Everything—the Universe, Infinity, all the galaxies, planets, every blade of grass, every stick and stone, every bird, insect—all Substance, all Form, all Activity. Oh, when I speak the word *God*, I feel I have said *Everything*. Yet I am sure that in some countries of the Far East the word *Allah* means just what the word *God* does to me, and there are some to whom the word *Brahman* means all the word *God* means to some of us. So it is clear the word *God* is not mandatory. What is of the utmost importance is the feeling we experience when we speak *any* word or combination of words that mean what God is, and All that God is.

There are some who experience this glorious Allness, Oneness, when they speak, hear, or read *Infinity*. To some, the word *Principle* brings this sense of loving, tender Allness. Recently, a very enlightened and sincere Identity said that *Celestial Energy* felt right to her, rather than the word *God*. And there are many who feel the Presence of God as they speak the word *Omnipresence*.

In answer to those of you who have asked whether or not it was wrong to use some other word than *God*, I can only speak as it is revealed. I do not feel it is wrong to use any word for God, so long as this word or combination of words brings the feeling of the Presence, the Oneness, the Love, the Allness that is God. No one can, or has a right to, tell you what the word *God* means to you. Just as all revelation must be Self-revelation, so it is that God can only be God to you in whatever word or words God reveals Himself to you in your own Consciousness. In other words, the word is not so important, but the feeling you experience when you speak the word or words is of the utmost importance.

Sometimes in the complete silence of deep contemplation, we find the word that means God to us almost silently speaking itself, and then there are no words at all. It is in the God-experience beyond words that the All that God is reveals Itself. This, Beloved, is full illumination. This is pure ecstasy. Truly, God is beyond words. But often the word *God* brings us to the full revelation of God, and thus, the point beyond words. Therefore, we will not be too concerned with words. But we will continue to be concerned with the absolute feeling of seeing, and being, the very Presence of that which is God, and nothing else or other.

There Is One Alone (Ecclesiastes 4:8)

So often, someone will say, "I just can't seem to make any connection between the Absolute Existence I experience in contemplation and the human existence I seem to experience."

This is not surprising because there is no connection between the Absolute Existence and the assumptive existence which is called the human experience. *There are not two experiences.* In fact, there cannot be two opposing experiences, or existences, because all Being is *one* infinite, indivisible, omnipresent Being. This fact precludes the possibility of two opposite existences. So long as it *seems* there is a human existence separate from, or other than, the infinite Existence, there is going to seem to be dualism.

There simply are no strictly human experiences. There are no born human beings to be conscious of any experience at all. Nonetheless, there is Something alive here. There is Something conscious here. There is Something intelligent and loving here. *Where* is this living, conscious, intelligent Love? It is right here where it appears there are born so-called human beings. *When* is the living, conscious, intelligent Love here? Right now, constantly, eternally. So we can rest assured that whatever is here, whatever is going on here and now, is an absolutely genuine Being, experiencing just what this eternal Being truly *is*.

There are some who try to reinterpret the so-called human being and his experiences. There can be neither interpretation nor reinterpretation. To attempt to interpret or reinterpret would be the pseudo activity attributed to a nonexistent born mind. In short, this would require a so-called mental effort, and the one indivisible Absolute Truth is *never* perceived in this fallacious way.

It is true that the *apparent* turmoil of the world enhances the seeming confusion of dualistic twoness. It is also true that even the apparently most evil situations and experiences are not at all what they seem to be. But again, there *is* something going on here. There is tremendous activity, surging and flowing throughout this entire planet Earth. Now the question arises, "But how can we avoid seeing and believing in a second world, a second existence, when it all seems to be so real, so opposite to that which we see in contemplation and illumination?"

Well, there is but one way, and this way is to actually see, perceive, that which is here, that which is alive here, and that which *is* going on right here and now. Certain it is that we cannot keep trying to "unsee" the apparent turmoil and trouble. Even if we could unsee such an illusion temporarily, it would return again and again. So the way is clear. Rather than trying to push something aside or to unsee it, we must be so absolutely positive of that which *is* here and that which *is* going on, here and now, that we realize there is nothing to be unseen, and neither is there anything that must be pushed aside.

So let us face the Absolute certain fact that there really is but *one* Existence and *One* who exists. When we say, "God is All, All is God," let us be very sure it means to perceive that *All is God*. This being true, where does this leave a second existence that is not God? Where does this leave a troubled, confused world? *Nowhere at all.* There is no such existence, and there is no such activity or experience. Furthermore, there is no one having such illusory experiences, and most important of all is the fact that there is no one conscious or aware of such experiences.

We have said we do not ignore that which seems to be evil. We never push it aside, nor do we honor it by trying to unsee it. What do we do? We face it, no matter how dark and forbidding it may *appear* to be. We look right at it, and then—oh then, Beloved—we actually see that which *is* here. We truly perceive that which is going on here. We are aware of the very Presence that is Absolute Perfection, Peace, Joy, Heaven, right here where the opposite to this Truth seems to be.

There really is one World, and we actually *see* the Substance that is alive, conscious, intelligent, loving, right here and now. *This is all we see.* We do not *try* to see the glorious Presence that is All there is here. We are just so aware of that which is here and that which is going on here that we are completely unaware of anything separate from, other than, or opposite to that which genuinely *is* right here.

Just now I feel impelled to mention a poem entitled "Omnipresence" in the book *Poems of the Ultimate*. [This poem has been included below—Ed.] This poem clearly reveals that, because God truly *is All*, this Existence right here and now is Heaven Itself. Someone has said, "Earth, when rightly perceived, is Heaven." This is true. You will recall that David, the Psalmist, said, "If I make my bed in hell, behold thou art there" (Ps. 139:8). No greater Truth could be stated. Yes, no matter how hopeless the fantasy may seem to be, God is right where the false picture seems to be, and because God is *All that is present*, there can be no hell at all. That which seemed to be hell was Heaven all the while.

All that is necessary, or ever was necessary, is to see it as it actually *is* and as it forever has been, and to acknowledge no other power or presence than God. Let us then "Stand fast therefore in the liberty wherewith Christ hath made us free, and be not entangled again with the yoke of bondage" (Gal. 5:1).

Yes, *now* we are completely free from all duality, from twoness, from otherness or opposites. We truly are the Christ, which is God being man. It is one eternal, constant Christ-Consciousness which is constantly aware of all things as they are. This Christ-Identity which you are knows nothing whatever of duality or indeed of *anything* separate from, other than, or opposite to God, the All being All.

We are not in bondage to nonexistent duality. We are not bound by a *kind* of mind, consciousness, that does not even exist. We know that so-called human activity, rightly perceived, is God in action. There is none other to act or to be. Thus it is everlastingly, and we are *That*.

Omnipresence

What is the heaven they deem
To be so far removed?
Where is this heaven they seem
To have to be reproved
And suffer, ere they enter
To the glory of its center?

Whence cometh vain illusion,
Deception and confusion?
What is it that deceiveth?
Who is it that believeth
That Heaven must be attained
Or more of God be gained
By deeds or pleading prayer?

Is God not All? Where could He be,
If not right here? And why would He
Seek or plead or search to know
Himself? Oh, All is God, and so
There is no seeker, no search here,
For Heaven's all that doth appear
When God is clearly seen to be
The only One called You, or Me.

Light and Love,
Marie S. Watts

May 1969

*In the beginning was the Word, and the Word was
with God, and the Word was God.*

—John 1:1

Dear One,

Again I must thank you for your many letters telling
of help, inspiration, and illumination as you continue to
study and contemplate the first volume of the 1968 classnotes. Some of you have reported glorious experiences
which the world would call miracles. But we know that
the miracle is ever-present as the constant, conscious
Perfection that we are.

Self-Revelation

The Ultimate Absolute is total Self-revelation. As
you know, the title of the textbook of our particular
approach is *The Ultimate*. However, the subtitle of this
book is *Your Self Revealed.* It is the subtitle of *The Ultimate*
that states the basic principle and the purpose of every
revelation that is presented in these writings.

As we have often stated, all revelation is Self-revelation.
This basic Principle of the Ultimate is Absolute Truth. No
one can be taught Absolute Truth. No one can learn Absolute Truth. No one can reveal Absolute Truth *to* you. No
reasoning or striving to understand the Truth you read or
hear will reveal this Absolute Truth *to* you. The *only* way
in which Absolute Truth can be known, really known, is
by conscious perception, and *you* are the Consciousness
that perceives this Truth. You are the Perceiver and the
Perception. But this is not all. You are also That which is
perceived. Once you are completely aware of this important

26

fact, you find that you are consciously *experiencing* Absolute Truth. Yes, you experience *being* this Truth.

Sometimes one will say, "I had an illumined experience" or, "It is necessary to have an illumined experience in order to actually perceive this Truth." Strictly speaking, no one really *has* this experience. Rather, he or she is aware of *being* the glorious experience and of being the one who experiences. In short, the revelatory experience and the experiencer are one and the same. However, this illumined experience never takes place when one is *trying* to concentrate, understand, or interpret that which you hear or read.

It is well to frequently consider Jesus' statement as recorded in John 6:45:

> It is written in the prophets, And they shall be all taught of God. Every man therefore that hath heard, and hath learned of the Father, cometh unto me.

Jesus well knew that Absolute Truth cannot be taught. He also knew that Self-revelation is the only way in which God, the eternal, infinite Christ, can be known, thus experienced. There is tremendous spiritual significance in the last sentence of the above quotation. Yes, every one of us who *really* hears is conscious of the Father *being* the Son, the Christ, and thus, he has come to an awareness of being the Christ. This is Self-revelation.

There are some sincere students of the Absolute Truth who sincerely object to the statement that "all revelation is Self-revelation." They are honestly convinced that teachers and students, leaders and followers, are necessary. Some of them will insist that because there have been students and teachers, leaders and followers, throughout the ages, they were, and are, essential to complete understanding. This seems to be particularly true of those who have considered themselves to be followers and students of metaphysical teachers and leaders. Then, sometimes, there seems to be a personal sense of love and loyalty to one specific teacher or leader.

All of this is understandable. Yet the fact remains that, as Jesus states, each one of us must ultimately experience his own Self-revelations and be his own Self-revelator. This, of course, means that finally the God, Christ-Being, we genuinely are does reveal Itself as the *only* Self, or Being, that exists or has ever existed. Yes, when we arrive at Self-revelation and clearly perceive that only in this way can we know what we are—thus, what God is—only then have we arrived at the Absolute Truth, which is our Christhood. Thus, we experience *being* that which we are, *all* that we are, and *only* that which we are.

So long as we continue to depend upon leaders and teachers for our spiritual perception, we are going to also delay our own complete awareness of *being* infinite Intelligence, Consciousness, Life, and Love. Any effort to concentrate upon the statements of Absolute Truth we are hearing or reading appears to act as a deterrent to Self-revelation. This is true because it would have to be an activity of the so-called born, or human, mind trying to control itself.

It is true that when we were immersed in the duality of metaphysics we did try to concentrate our attention upon what we considered the words of Truth. But the Ultimate Absolute is not metaphysics. There is no duality in the complete *Oneness* that is Absolute Truth, and having arrived at the Ultimate Absolute, we can no longer proceed from a dualistic standpoint. But oh, the sheer joy we experience when all effort of assumptive mind is transcended and we experience our Christ, or God, Self revealing Itself *to* Itself *as* Itself. Only in this way can we know and *know* that we know.

Right here I feel impelled to quote from a letter I received a few days ago:

I have been studying diligently, but without trying to think about that which I read. At first it seemed difficult not to stop and "work" or think. But it surely is the right way because now I find that when I least expect it, wonderful revelations come, and I just let them flow. One revelation that came was: serene and imperturbable Mind am I. Consciousness is never separated into "I" and "others." Consciousness is One Whole Completeness and is never separated or disturbed.

Isn't this wonderful? Here is the Self, revealing Itself in Its *own* way and in Its own words. And just recently a letter came from Alaska in which there were so many wonderful Absolute Truths revealed and stated in words and statements that she probably had never read or heard. My Heart leapt with Joy. Oh, so many letters are received telling of wonderful Self-revelation. Each day brings greater gratitude and Joy.

Self-revelation is only experienced when the Consciousness is "full open." We are aware of being full open Consciousness when there is no effort to understand or interpret the words of Truth we are hearing or reading. This does not mean that the Mind, Intelligence, is inactive. Intelligence is *ever* active, for It is omniactive Mind Itself. Certain it is that we are aware of that which we are hearing or reading. But we are not making any mental effort to fathom or interpret the meaning of the words we hear or read. Rather, we listen, we read for the sheer Joy of experiencing the Truths that are far beyond any words that could be spoken or written about these Absolute Truths. At least for a while, the words do fulfill a certain purpose. But it is not until we are consciously beyond *any* words that full, complete Self—God—revelation is experienced.

When we view a beautiful sunset or sunrise, we never try to analyze the "contents" of this Beauty. We never try to interpret it, nor do we attempt to reason as to what it means. When we read beautiful poetry or gaze raptly at a work of art, we do not try to dissect it or analyze it. To do so would defeat the purpose of the Beauty Itself. When we listen to beautiful music, we do not analyze it, nor do we try to interpret it. This is true, although we may have studied and performed this music for what the world calls years and can analyze and interpret it. But to really *hear* the Absolute Beauty that is our own Consciousness, we must have transcended all effort to analyze or to interpret. Just as we are the Beauty that we see, so it is that we are the Beauty that we hear.

Absolute Perfection is Beauty. Eternal, constant, living, intelligent, conscious Love is this same Beauty. Infinite, indivisible Oneness is constant, eternal Omnipresence and Beauty. In Biblical terminology, when we see with the single eye and when we hear with what Jesus called that "other ear," we are truly seeing, we are truly hearing. And that which we are seeing and hearing, we are experiencing.

This, beloved One, is Self-revelation, and the Self revealed is the Self experienced. Thus, we are aware that *we are* every Absolute Truth we ever hear or read. The Bible states, "Before they call I will answer." Yes, before we ever read one word of Absolute Truth, we *were* this Truth. Before we ever heard one word of Absolute Truth, we were that Truth. There is no time. So that which we were, we *are*. That which we will be, we are. Self-revelation is the Absolute Ultimate Truth, revealing and manifesting Itself as the I AM that is God, thus, the *I* that you are. There is no other for you to be.

In Light and Love,
Marie S. Watts

June 1969

In the beginning was the Word, and the Word was with God, and the Word was God.
—John 1:1

Dear One,

These are indeed happy days. The sheer joy of constant, glorious, ever greater revelation is beyond description. But then, I know you do understand because you too are constantly experiencing ever greater revelations. The glory of these revelations is that they are the Consciousness that You are, revealing Itself to Itself, *as* Itself.

From the reports I am receiving, it is obvious that many of you will be attending our coming symposium. Now I can tell you that I am so glad the word *symposium* was revealed. The word *class* has always had a connotation of teacher *and* student. This would mean that something was being taught, and of course, we know that in the Ultimate Absolute there can be no teacher, no student, and certainly this Absolute Truth cannot be taught *to* anyone. Our glorious revelatory experiences are completely Self-revelatory, and above all, they are completely free from twoness, otherness, or duality of any kind.

Among Webster's definitions of the word *symposium*, we find the following: "a conference organized for the discussion of some particular subject." Certain it is that this definition has no connotation of teacher and student. Of course, we do visibly meet, and we do discuss this absolute, complete, impersonal Truth. But our discussion is *not* audible. Neither is it an exchange of so-called intellectual or human opinions. The audible words can never reveal this Absolute Truth *to* anyone. Rather, it is the *one* indivisible Consciousness gloriously revealing Itself *as* the only Consciousness of each and every one of us. This wonderful revelatory experience can only be because we are all *one inseparable, full open Consciousness.*

And now, beloved One, the Light is a constant, indescribable experience. You are the Experience; You are the Experiencer; for You are the Light Itself.

Here Is Everywhere, Everywhere Is Here

As you know, a landing on the moon is scheduled for next month. It is Love in action for us to be fully aware of, and as, this experience. From the standpoint of that which is called the world, this trip to and from the moon is supposed to be fraught with danger. So let us perceive the Absolute Truth pertaining to this scheduled experience.

Are these courageous astronauts going anywhere that is separate and apart from the infinite, omnipresent Consciousness that they are, right here, right now? No! Can any one of us really go anywhere that is outside of, or other than, the infinite, indivisible, ever intelligent, loving, living Consciousness that we are? No! Where does our infinite awareness of being begin? *Nowhere.* Where does it end? *Nowhere.* Where is there a circumference or a boundary line that confines any one if us? *Nowhere.* Consciousness is eternally, infinitely unconfined.

When Columbus set sail for what had been called the New World, it was believed the Earth was flat and that at a certain boundary line his ships must inevitably drop right off the Earth. Thus, it was believed that the ships, and all those aboard the ships, would perish or be destroyed. Certain it is that the success of the trip was very much in doubt, and there must have been much fear. Well, we know the answers to that particular episode. There was, and is, no dropping-off place. There was no circumference beyond which lay destruction or oblivion. There was no vacuum into which they could disappear.

Now, this same Truth is true with, and as, our astronauts. Let us now go beyond the so-called world opinion concerning the coming experience and perceive the actual Absolute Truth that is revealing Itself as this entire activity. How does it happen that Columbus refused to be confined to just one small segment of the Earth planet? How does it come about that our astrophysicists as well as our astronauts refuse to be confined to this tiny dot in infinity that is called the planet Earth?

Beloved, this entire so-called space effort is due to one glorious fact: inherently we know that we are *infinite*, unconfined, unlimited. Some of us may not seem, as yet, to be fully aware that we *know* our inseparable, boundless Infinitude. Nonetheless, this awareness has to be the very Consciousness that *is* conscious as each and every one of us. Our Consciousness is as unlimited and unconfined as is our boundless Universe, even as our Universe is as boundless and unconfined as is our Consciousness. It is this inherent knowledge that insists upon refusing to be limited, bound, or confined. Furthermore, we are inherently aware of the fact that there are, and can be, no vacuums in and as the infinite, boundless Consciousness that we are.

Where could we go that we're not already? Since we are indivisibly boundless, where could we go that would be outside of, or other than, the Consciousness we are? There will, of course, come a day when it will no longer even seem to be necessary to *go* anywhere in order to be conscious of being focalized at, and as, any and every focalization of our infinite, boundless Being. Thus, of course, there will be no necessity for us to travel in spaceships or to even *seem* to be faced with danger. But actually, there is no time, so right now we can realize that all that is ever to be known is known right *now*. Thus, there is no knowledge of danger, and there can be *no one who is aware of being in danger.* All that has ever been *is* right now. All that will ever be *is* right now. It is in, and as, this absolute, complete Consciousness that our boys live and move and experience the entirety of their Being.

This is an intelligent Universe. It is omniactive Intelligence acting intelligently as every focalization of Itself. Intelligent activity always acts as perfect order and balance. Not one iota of this perfect, intelligent Omniaction can ever depart from Its right orbit. Consider the heavens. What is it that holds the stars and planets in their proper orbit? What is it that supports these heavenly Bodies? From all appearance, there is nothing solid as a support for even one star or planet.

Oh, beloved One, it is the very same omnipotent Omnipresence that supports *all* Substance in form, and it matters not what specific form this Substance may be. *The Substance, the Form, and That which supports it are all one and the same. It is absolute, omnipotent, intelligent, conscious Love.*

This is the inseparable Oneness we so often mention. It is Consciousness conscious of being this indivisible, omnipotent *Love.* Love holds everything right where it belongs, but this Love does not confine anything. Orbiting in and as any specific fulfillment of purpose, such as being held in a right orbit, does not separate, nor does it confine, the Substance in form called a star, a planet, or a spaceship. A star, a planet, or a spaceship is but that particular focalization of the one infinite, omnipresent All.

For every Absolute Truth, we can find confirmation of this Truth in our beloved Bible. Speaking of the indivisible Omnipresence of Consciousness, let us consider what David had to say (I have quoted this Psalm before, but it is so apropos, I shall again refer to it:

> Whither shall I go from thy Spirit? or whither shall I flee from thy presence? (Ps. 139:7).

Spirit and Consciousness are the same thing. Spirit *is* Consciousness, even as Consciousness *is* Spirit. Now, where could anyone go that would separate him from the God, Christ, Consciousness that he eternally, constantly is? He can no more be separate from this everlasting Consciousness than he can be separate from himself. This is true because his Consciousness *is* the Self that he is. Then how could he go or be anywhere that would not be the very Presence of the Christ-Consciousness that he eternally is?

Then David continues:

> If I ascend up into heaven, thou art there (Ps. 139:8).

Oh yes, Heaven *is* everywhere, for Heaven is *the* Everywhere. Where God, Heaven, *is*—and God is everywhere—Heaven is. Thus, as David said:

> If I take the wings of the morning, and dwell in the uttermost parts of the sea; Even there shall thy hand lead me; and thy right hand shall hold me (Ps. 139:9-10).

Oh, beloved One, this is *Love*. It is well to contemplate this Omnipresence that is Love when you are consciously aware of our courageous astronauts.

Now I would like to mention another passage from our beloved Bible which has meant much to me in diverse, seeming dangerous situations:

> He shall cover thee with his feathers, and under his wings shalt thou trust (Ps. 91:4).

Here again, we find omnipresent, omniactive, inseparable Love to be the *Power* and the *Presence*. There are many statements in our precious Bible that point to the protective Omnipresence that is Love. Among them, you will find the following inspiring statement:

The eternal God is thy refuge, and underneath are the everlasting arms (Deut. 33:27).

Here again, we find the tender, loving Presence that is All Presence everywhere, for it is *the* Everywhere. I cannot tell you how great has been the power of the Absolute Truth and Love evidenced in verses from Romans:

For I am persuaded, that neither death, nor life, nor angels, nor principalities, nor powers, nor things present, nor things to come, Nor height, nor depth, nor any other creature, shall be able to separate us from the love of God, which is in Christ Jesus our Lord (Rom. 8:38-39).

If the foregoing quotations from our Bible were to be considered from an orthodox standpoint, they would certainly seem to be completely dualistic. But considered from the standpoint of the Absolute, they do reveal the indivisible Allness, the eternal, omnipresent Oneness, that is All Being.

There are so many glorious statements of Absolute Truth in our Bible, and now that we recognize the true significance of these statements, they are literally fraught with Power.

Beloved, Love is Power, and without Love there could be no Power; without Love there would be nothing. God truly is All. And God is Love, even as Love is God.

Light and Love,
Marie S. Watts

July 1969

*In the beginning was the Word, and the Word was
with God, and the Word was God.*

—*John 1:1*

Dear One,

It is with great joy that we are anticipating our coming
symposium. Many of you will be with us, and of course,
we are so happy that you are to attend.

Some of you have questioned as to why we have called
our coming meeting a "symposium." Well, I have never
liked the word *class* very well, as it has a connotation of
teacher *and* student association. Strictly speaking, our
meetings have never really been classes. How could they,
when there was no one *teaching* anything?

There seemed to be a need for another term for these
revelatory experiences, so of course, the right word
appeared. One of Webster's definitions for *symposium* is:
"Any meeting where ideas are freely exchanged." Well, of
course, we do not exactly exchange ideas. But we certainly
do experience a beautiful Oneness, in which the revelations
of each one of us are the revelations of all. In any event,
this word *symposium* is a better word by far for our purpose
than is the word *class*. Many of you are very happy with
this word, and of course, this enhances our happiness that
it has been revealed.

Consciousness Is Substance

Perhaps the greatest seeming block to our complete
awareness of Oneness lies in the fact that we do not fully
realize that Consciousness is Substance. In fact, it is the
only Substance. We speak and write about the atom, the

nucleus, etc., but all the while we are speaking and writing of Consciousness, and the Substance that is Consciousness is eternally, constantly, inseparably *One*. We look at a tree, and because the Substance that is the tree *seems* to be a solid, separate substance, we consider the tree to be a separate substance of and by itself. This simply is not true. The Substance that is the tree is the one infinite, indivisible Substance which is Consciousness.

When we see this tree, *really* see it, we clearly perceive that the Substance in form called tree is none other than the one *All*—indivisible, universal Substance. We see this Substance in form, and we identify it as tree. But generally, we mistakenly see this tree as a separate material substance. Yet even our apparent misconception of the tree cannot separate it from the indivisible, infinite Substance which it *is*.

There is no such thing as an inactive Consciousness. Consciousness is always in motion. Indeed, Consciousness *is* Activity. We perceive this activity and we call it Life. And *Life it is*. This is why Consciousness is Activity Itself. You see, Life *is* Activity, even as Activity is Life. Without Life, there could be no activity, and without Activity, there could be no Life. The Activity, Life, which exists as that which we call the tree exists *everywhere*. It *is* the Everywhere. It is completely indivisible. It does not exist as something separate just because It is identified in form and we call it tree.

From the foregoing, it is clear that Consciousness and Life are one and the same Essence. There is no inactive Consciousness, nor is there an unconscious activity. Living Consciousness is *conscious* Life, and conscious Life is living Consciousness. This is a *living* Universe. It is alive. This living, conscious Universe is one completely inseparable and omniactive Essence, and everything in existence consists of this *inseparable* Essence.

More and more, the astrophysicists are aware of the fact that this is a purposeful Universe. Just recently, some of them perceived that it is an intelligent Universe. *Of course It is intelligent.* How else, or in what other way, could it be Its infinite, complete fulfillment of purpose? We just *must* stop this thing of considering this Universe as though It were merely an unintelligent, mechanical robot sort of thing. It isn't, you know. The Intelligence which *is* this Universe is everywhere. It is *the* Everywhere. It is as inseparable as is living Consciousness, or conscious Life. Indeed, It *is* living Intelligence. It is conscious Life. It acts intelligently; It acts purposefully, and It is a constant fulfillment of Its purpose. It is conscious. It is alive. It is intelligent because it is Intelligence. *And we call it Mind.*

So now we perceive that this Universe consists of conscious, living Mind; living, conscious Intelligence; and conscious, intelligent Life. And of course, the Life is the eternal, constant, indivisible Activity that is this Universe in ceaseless action. Indeed, living, intelligent Consciousness is the hereness and the nowness of *all that Mind knows*. It is the complete, inseparable, universal knowledge, or knowing, and as stated before, the conscious knowing is the Activity, or the Life.

When we look at that Essence in form that we call tree, this is what we are really seeing. But is this all we are seeing? *No, it is not.* The most important Fact of all Existence has not been mentioned, and of course, this Fact is *Love.* Without Love, this would be a terrible universe. Without Love, this Universe would be separated into bits and parts of Itself, and these bits and parts would be constantly warring against each other. Then we would have something like that which our pseudo world picture would have us believe today. But this Universe is *not* a separable universe. Why? Because It is Love.

Love is the Power that maintains and sustains the complete inseparability that is this Universe. It is not that Love acts as a sort of cement or gravity that holds so-called separate bits and parts of this Universe together. Not at all is it like this. *Love is the Essence that is this Universe. This is a loving Universe.* It has to be loving because it is Love.

There is no unconscious Love. Love is conscious, so It is Consciousness Itself. There is no unintelligent Love; Love is intelligent, so It *is* Intelligence. There is no inactive, or dead, Love. Love *is* Activity. Activity is Life. So Love is Life Itself. So, Beloved, we perceive that this Universe consists of conscious, living, intelligent Love. But It also consists of intelligent, conscious, loving Life. Mind, actively knowing every Truth, or Fact, *is* the conscious, intelligent, loving activity of this indivisible Essence.

Yes, Love is the indivisible Oneness of the entire Essence that is this Universe. Love is the eternal, intelligent Peace that is this inseparable Universe. Love is the constant, intelligent knowing that is *all* Knowledge. Above all, *Love is the Power that is this Universe.* Love *is* Power. Without Love, Power would indeed be a totally evil thing (if there were such a thing as evil). But indeed, *all Power is Love.* There is no Power that is not Love and no Love that is not Power.

Love is eternal. It does not begin, nor can It end. Love is immutable. It cannot change. Love is steady and always even. It does not fluctuate. Love is Perfection; always It is perfect. There is no such thing as imperfect Love. Love is always lovely and beautiful. It is Beauty Itself. *There is nothing ugly under the sun.*

Now we perceive that Life, Consciousness, Intelligence —Mind—and Love are *one and the same Essence*, and this Essence, Beloved, is the *only* Substance in existence. It is this Substance that is the perfect, omnipresent Beauty that is this gloriously beautiful Universe.

This inseparable Beauty manifests Itself in and as innumerable shades and tones. It is Music. It is Art. It is the sunrise and the sunset. It is the dew on the grass. It is the very Essence in form of everything and everyone. It is here inseparably, but in the form of a symphony. It is here inseparably, but in the form of a beautiful painting. It is here indivisibly, in and as the Substance in form of a rose, a seashell, a poem, or a tree. It is here in and as color and form as the butterfly, the bird, or the serpent. Oh yes, It is here in an innumerable variety of forms and colors.

It is this infinite variety of delineations that comprises the Beauty that is this Universe. If there were not variety, there could be no Beauty. If there were but one color, there could be no Beauty. If there were but one tone, there could be no Music. If there were but one rhythmic tempo, there could never be the Beauty of the ballet, the Beauty of the Music, Art, or of this ever active, orderly, balanced Universe Itself.

Beloved One, does it seem to you that this article has been cold, a purely scientific article? Well, what have we been talking about here? What *is* all of this indivisible Substance, Form, and activity we have been discussing? It is God, God, God. Indeed, what else or other than God is there to talk about? Nothing at all. Just God—that is All.

In Light and Love,
Marie S. Watts

August 1969

In the beginning was the Word, and the Word was
with God, and the Word was God.

—John 1:1

Dear One,

Words can never describe the glory that was, and is, revealed as our symposium was experienced. And the experience is still going on. It will continue to be our experience in ever greater Light and glory ad infinitum.

Almost constantly, the rooms were a blaze of brilliant Light. Of course, this was due to the fact that those who were visibly present were, and are, the Light Itself. And the Love—oh, the Love was felt and even seen so powerfully that it was indeed beautiful. Almost everyone was aware of the glorious Light. To some, It manifested Itself as great shafts of Light crossing and re-crossing the room. To some, It was one indivisible Presence. To some, It varied from session to session. But above all, It was experienced by most of those who attended. We know that not one of us can ever even *seem* to be what and where we were spiritually before this wonderful experience.

Throughout our nation and world, many Identities were listening in. Now calls are coming in, telling of the revelations experienced by those who were full open Consciousness but were not visibly at the symposium. And glory be—their revelations for the most part are basically the same as were our revelations. Isn't it wonderful! Herein is the evidence that the one indivisible Consciousness that *is* all Existence is consciously everywhere because it *is* the Everywhere. Thus, the revelations experienced during our symposium were, and are, experienced throughout our nation and the world.

At the beginning of the Thursday morning session, we deliberately paused and were conscious of being everywhere and of being *the* Everywhere. We were specifically aware of being the Consciousness of everyone who was listening in and that everyone who was listening in was *our* Consciousness. Thus, we were aware of the fact that the Truths we were aware of seeing and being, You, who were not visibly present, were aware of seeing and being. But this is not all. We were aware that the Truths You were seeing and being, we were seeing and being. Oh, it was, and continues to be, so very beautiful.

Of course, this was not something that was planned. Infinite, living, conscious Love simply revealed Itself in this way, so of course, it has to be right and a tremendous fulfillment of purpose. All we can say is, Oh, glory be! *God really is All, All really is God.* And in order to be, to exist at all, we have to be *That* and nothing else, or other, at all. Thus, we are fully aware of the certain fact that there is no duality. Rather, there is *only the one infinite, indivisible All, which is God Being.*

We clearly and fully realize that our experience is your experience, even as your experience is our experience, for we are one indivisible Consciousness, and our inseparable Oneness is infinite, eternal *Love* Itself.

Dualism Transcended

Every problem that anyone ever *seems* to experience is due to the fallacy called dualism. Of course, the basis of this entire deception is that there is God and something that is not God. The illusion of duality is indeed subtle. Even though we are convinced that we have completely transcended all duality, this fallacy will continue to present itself at any unguarded moment, and it is necessary to be alert to the deceptive *appearance* of all twoness, or otherness, other than God and God alone.

In our Bible, there are many and various similes presented which tell of the necessity of being alert to supposed duality. As you know, many of the statements in our Bible are symbolic. We find a very fine symbolic simile in the Book of Nehemiah. When Nehemiah perceived that the wall of Jerusalem was broken down and the gates thereof burned, he knew that the wall must be rebuilt. However, the people among whom he lived were bitterly opposed to the rebuilding of the wall. This opposition did not deter Nehemiah, who felt divinely impelled to rebuild and repair the wall:

> Now it came to pass, when Sanballat, and Tobiah, and Geshem the Arabian, and the rest of our enemies, heard that I had builded the wall, and that there was no breach left therein; (though at that time I had not set up the doors upon the gates;)
> That Sanballat and Geshem sent unto me, saying, Come, let us meet together in some one of the villages in the plain of Ono. But they thought to do me mischief.
> And I sent messengers unto them saying, I am doing a great work, so that I cannot come down: why should the work cease, whilst I leave it, and come down to you?
> Yet they sent unto me four times after this sort; and I answered them after the same manner (Neh. 6:1-4).

The foregoing quotation is a wonderful simile of the frequency and the subtlety of the appearance of fallacious duality. It also clearly depicts the necessity for us to be ever alert to its deception. But this does not mean we should by any means consider it as though it were something real or genuine. *There really is no duality, for God truly is all, and there is none else or other*. Yet the pseudo world of appearance would certainly convince us, if it could, that duality existed and that it really was, and is, a presence and power that we must recognize.

Before we *seemed* to be overtaken by the fallacy called birth, our freedom from all duality was complete. Thus, our wall of defense was secure. Yet as we *appeared* to become more and more enmeshed in the so-called world of duality, this defense seemed to crumble and to break down. Even as Nehemiah realized the necessity to rebuild the wall for the defense of his people, so it is that we have recognized the necessity to rebuild the wall of defense— or to transcend all false sense of duality. We truly have perceived the complete falsity of duality, and we have transcended its so-called deception.

It is noteworthy, however, that Nehemiah had not yet "set up the doors upon the gates." Perhaps we too may not yet have set up the doors upon the gates. So it does sometimes seem that the deceptive appearance called duality can occasionally find a temporary entrance. But we do not continue to permit this fallacy to occupy the premises of our Consciousness. We very quickly discern its mischief-making propensities and promptly dismiss it from our Consciousness. Actually, it never enters the God-Consciousness that we are. It is only in the *seeming* world of appearance that it even pretends to exist. Of and as itself, it can do nothing, for it is nothing. But we know that ultimately, we will have "set up the doors upon the gates," and the deception called dualism will not even *seem* to bring itself to our attention.

We too are engaged in a great work. We are the infinite Consciousness being the fulfillment of Its infinite, yet specific, purpose. Why should we come down to fraternize with apparent duality? We will not be deceived by a suppositional mind other than God.

Nonetheless, we must recognize the many ways in which this deception of duality can seem to present itself. One of the most frequent and subtle forms of this pretense to being is the suggestion that a mind other than God exists. This deceptive suggestion can apparently argue that this pseudo mind is evil and malicious and can be harmful to us. (We used to call it malpractice; now we know there is neither malpractice nor a malpractitioner.) But we cannot fear a kind of mind that does not exist. Rather, we can realize that the one and only Mind is the one indivisible God Itself. The very moment we perceive the complete Allness that is God, the duality of a suppositional intelligence is completely transcended.

Oh, there are innumerable ways in which fictional duality can seem to appear. It can seem to argue that there are separate persons who are antagonistic to each other. It can seem to present a picture of separate nations who must war against each other. It can seem to tell us we have separate friends and enemies. It can seem to present a picture of good *and* evil, perfection *and* imperfection, Truth *and* falsity. But we are not deceived. We *know* that the Absolute Truth we know, and are, is one indivisible, infinite All, and we stand and stand and stand, in and as that knowledge.

We know there is no separate, or other, person to judge or to be judged. We know just what Jesus meant when he lovingly said, "Judge not, that ye be not judged" (Matt. 7:1). We know there is but one infinite, inseparable Identity that is, or can be, identified as anyone or anything. Above all, we know that this inseparable Identity is God revealing, identifying, and manifesting Himself as each and every one of us. Truly we *are* the Absolute Truth which is God, for there is nothing else, or other, for us to be.

Light and Love,
Marie S. Watts

September 1969

In the beginning was the Word, and the Word was
with God, and the Word was God.
—John 1:1

Dear One,

It is noteworthy that from your letters it is apparent that the revelations are taking place and being revealed in and as the words that flow as the Consciousness You are. This is proof positive that you are truly experiencing your own revelations. The words are innumerable in which these revelations are heard. It is apparent that each Identity must experience not only his own revelations, but they must also be in the words that are specifically revealed as his own Consciousness. Of course, this does not mean that a specific identity exists as a separate Consciousness. But it does mean that the infinite, indivisible Consciousness is identified as each and every specific Identity, and the words in which Self-revelation is experienced must inevitably be those that are heard and *experienced* as the Consciousness of each specific, but unseparated, identity.

But this is not all. Always, new words are being heard and experienced. There simply is no limit to the words in which Self-revelation is realized and experienced. For instance, since the writings of the Ultimate were first published in 1957, the terminology of these writings has constantly been ever new.

Now of course, the words of many of the earlier writings of the Ultimate are in quite common usage in the publications and in the conversations of those who write and speak somewhat in the Absolute terminology. But it is true that, with common usage, words seem to become meaningless. We may read them and hear them, but they tend to become just words to us. This fact, Beloved, is why it is of the utmost necessity that new words constantly be revealed as our own revelations. So of course, when letters come in reporting the revelations You are experiencing, in the *words* that are being revealed as your Consciousness, my Heart really rejoices.

Beloved, today many of us truly perceive the Universe and this planet Earth as It *is*. Yet the "prince of this world" still appears. Although we truly see the glory that is this Heaven, we continue to recognize the pseudo appearance of a *kind* of world that does not exist. Yet no matter how terrible it may *appear* to be, it finds no response whatever in or as our Consciousness. It may appear to be separate nations, peoples filled with hatred and at war with each other. But *we know better*. We know the Heaven that *is* this Earth. It may appear to be birth, age, and death, but the "prince of this world" does not deceive us. It may appear to be poverty or dishonesty, but it finds no response within and as the Consciousness that we are.

Oh yes, the prince of this world can seem to present itself as fear, worry, dread, etc., but we *know* there is never anything to fear and that there is no Mind, Intelligence, that is aware of worry or foreboding. We know that truly All is Peace and Joy.

Does this mean we completely ignore those who seem to be in trouble? No! We *love* because we *are* Love. Thus, we have compassion, even as did Jesus. We know full well just how real the so-called prince of this world can seem to be. But we also know that to respond to it as though it really existed would never help anyone to transcend its deception. So with all of our compassion, *Love*, we do not "come down" to the seeming problems. Rather, we remain completely aware of the uninterrupted Heaven that *is* here. In this way only can we be the Light of the world.

You will recall that Jesus clearly stated:

> Ye are the light of the world. A city that is set on an hill cannot be hid ... Let your light so shine before men, that they may see your good works, and glorify your Father which is in heaven (Matt. 5:14,16).

Yes, truly, we *are* the Light that lights the seeming darkness of a pseudo world of inharmony. Thus, if sickness, pain, or *any appearance* of inharmony should be presented, we do not consider it as something that really exists and that must be overcome. Rather, we just do not respond to it, nor do we believe it at all. *We know the Heaven that is.*

"The Prince of This World Cometh"

The complete quotation of the above title is:

> Hereafter I will not talk much with you: for the prince of this world cometh, and hath nothing in me (John 14:30).

When Jesus spoke these meaningful words, he realized that he was nearing the end of his visible fulfillment of purpose as far as those who were *considered* to be his followers were concerned. Yes, he had arrived at that complete realization in which the "prince" of this world continued to present itself but found absolutely no response in, or as, the Christ-Consciousness which he was and is. Beloved, it is the entire fallacious picture of a universe, a world, a creation, called man or whatever, separate from, or other than, God, the *only*, the infinite *All*.

The glorious One called Jesus had faced, and even seemed to experience to some extent, the entire fallacious misconception of a temporary world inhabited by a temporary born, or created, existence. You will recall that even this blessed One was *supposed* to have been born. (Even though the church represented him as having been immaculately conceived, he was supposedly born.) He was supposed to appear as a baby body, then the body of a boy, and then as the mature so-called man, even as it has appeared that we were babies, then children, youths, and finally so-called mature, aging, and aged beings.

It is not surprising that Jesus said, "Hereafter I will not talk much with you." He knew that mere words could never reveal *to anyone* the glorious, absolute, infinite Truth which he was seeing and being. Jesus well knew that from this point on the disciples, and all with whom he had talked, must experience their own revelations. He also knew that if these revelations were revealed in or as words, the words would have to be those which were revealed as the Consciousness of each and every Identity.

But there is another aspect of Self-revelation which was exceedingly clear in and as the Consciousness of the one called Jesus. He knew that generally the Self-revelation was not apparent in or as words at all. He clearly perceived that the Light which comprises omnipresent Infinity was, and is, the Light that "lighteth every man that cometh into the world" (John 1:9). He well knew, and knows, the futility of any attempt to describe this Universe or this Earth planet in words.

You see, Jesus was completely aware of the actual Heaven that *is* right here and everywhere. Even so, Jesus perceived that the world of appearance did seem to exist and that this pseudo world did seem to be the genuine and only world to supposedly born man. Thus, he plainly said, "The prince of this world cometh." However, Jesus was not deceived. Even though darkness—ignorance, absence of knowledge—did present itself, it found absolutely no response in or as the Consciousness of the glorious Christ Jesus

Again, and again during our so-called classes, we have spoken of the necessity to be "full open Consciousness." Sometimes someone will inquire as to just what it means to be "full open Consciousness." Well, it truly means to attach no genuine significance to the *words* that are spoken or heard, but just let the Consciousness be completely free and open, in order that the Absolute Truth being expressed beyond and between the words may reveal Itself in any way that really is *your* revelation. This, Beloved, is the only way in which you can be absolutely positive that you *are* the revelation and that you are the revelator.

You will recall that Jesus often spoke in parables. Certain it is that he did not expect his hearers to attempt to analyze or interpret the words he was speaking. Rather, he just encouraged those who heard him to consider the Absolute Truths that existed between and beyond the words. In short, he was inviting them to be full open Consciousness in order that they might experience their own revelations.

Actually, all the words that can be spoken, heard, or written, as far as the Truth is concerned, are in reality *One Word*, and this is the Word that is spoken in John 1:1, "In the beginning was the Word, and the Word was with God, and the Word was God."

Of course, there is no beginning, so the eternal Word is the eternal God. It has be this way, Beloved, because there is nothing else or other to say or even to talk about. Yes, again and again we say, "God is All, All is God." But actually, just the one word, *God*, is all that is required. You see, this is true because all revelation is God revealing, God identifying, and God manifesting as *just what God eternally is.* Therefore, to be full open Consciousness means to be aware of God (yes, even *as* God) and God alone. Actually, there is nothing existing that we can know or perceive separate from, or other than, God.

Now, all the foregoing does not mean we should not read, speak, or hear the words in which Absolute Truth is revealed. What it does mean is that no matter what may be the words we speak, hear, or read, we fully recognize that the words are merely sounds or symbols that signify the omnipresent, constant Eternality that is God being All, All being God. Yet even though we speak in this vein, we do recognize that even the sounds and the symbols have to be God revealing Itself, or there can be no sounds or symbols.

Above all, never let us mistake the sounds or the symbols we read or hear for our own Self-revelation, in which God so beautifully reveals Itself, or Himself, to be the entirety of our infinite, yet specific, Being.

Light and Love,
Marie S. Watts

October 1969

*In the beginning was the Word, and the Word was
with God, and the Word was God.*

—John 1:1

Dear One,

Your letters continue to come in, telling of glorious revelations. How truly wonderful it is that this Light is being experienced by those of you who reside in so many nations of the world. Truly, the one indivisible Consciousness, which is Love, is being revealed and evidenced, and we *know* that Love is Power.

If we accepted and believed the reports from the *apparent* world and nation today, we would surely conclude that hatred, strife, chicanery, and complete confusion were indeed rampant. It is imperative that we perceive the indivisible Nature of that Absolute Truth which is *Love*. Love is an inseparable, ever-present Essence, and because Love, Life, Intelligence, Consciousness are *one and the same Essence*, all Existence consists of this inseparable Essence. If this omnipresent Essence did not exist, there certainly could not even *seem* to be an opposite to Its Essence. All that portrays itself as division, hatred, strife, etc., only signifies the Presence of our indivisible Oneness, which is Love.

Beloved, here we stand, and the Love that we are is the *Power* in which we abide. Of course, the entire spurious picture can only appear to be presented because the illusion of duality does not seem to be completely transcended. Yet we know that because All really *is* God, there truly is no duality. Furthermore, there are no separate, born, dual minds to be hoodwinked by duality. The very word *dualism* has a connotation of separateness, twoness, etc. An illumined experience *always* reveals the complete, inseparable Oneness which is God, and God is Love.

If we say we must overcome the apparent strife and hatred of the world, we are saying that it—hatred, separateness—exists *as* something and that we are to overpower it or banish it from the world. It is impossible to overcome something which does not exist. Actually, it is impossible to overcome anything. *God is All*, and God can never be overcome. Such nonsense would mean that God must overcome Itself. So let us be through with this meaningless word *overcome*. All that is ever necessary is that our Awareness of Existence as It *is* be complete. In this Awareness of Existence completely, there is *only* inseparable Love, Peace, Joy, and *All that God is*. This complete awareness is realized and manifested as full open Consciousness reveals the Universe, the World, and all Substance, Form, and Activity to be *God* and *God alone*.

There is a well-known statement that says, "United we stand, divided we fall." This is good, but we must see further than that statement implies. We perceive that as *one* indivisible Love, we stand. Therefore, it is impossible for us to fall. We know that Love knows no separation; Love knows no otherness. Love knows only Its inseparable Self, which is Love *being*.

The Fallacy of the Antichrist

It is interesting to note that Jesus said nothing about the Antichrist. However, in 1 John we read:

> Little children, it is the last time: and as ye have heard that antichrist shall come, even now are there many antichrists; whereby we know that it is the last time ... Who is a liar but he that denieth that Jesus is the Christ? He is antichrist, that denieth the Father and the Son. Whosoever denieth the Son, the same hath not

the Father: but he that acknowledgeth the Son hath the Father also (1 John 2:18, 22-23).

Through the centuries there have been many, and there still are many, who deny that Jesus the Christ really existed. There are many who would deny that the Identity who was given the name Jesus the Christ exists as a living, moving, conscious Being right today. Nevertheless, there are many of us who know that Jesus the Christ did exist—and does exist—and we know *why* it is true.

And this is the promise that he hath promised us, even eternal life (1 John 2:25).

Yes, the eternal Christ-Life which was, and is, alive as the one they call Jesus is the very same Christ-Life that is alive as every Identity. Webster defines the Antichrist as "One who denies or opposes Christ." The prefix *anti* represents opposition, therefore, it stems from the word *opposite*. Thus, if there truly could be one who opposes Christ, this would have to be the very opposite of the Christ whom he was opposing.

As stated above, he who denies the Son has also denied the Father, and to deny the Christ is to deny the God-Consciousness that man genuinely *is*. Thus, to deny the Christ is to deny the Self. But to recognize, accept, and acknowledge *being* the Christ means to consciously be the Christ-Consciousness which is God.

It is not surprising that we have the promise of eternal Life, and we realize that we *are* Life eternal. Unless we exist as the God Christ Consciousness, we do not exist at all. Webster also defines the Antichrist as "a pretender to Christhood; a false Christ." A pretender to Christhood could never be the Christ. The Christ-Man is the *only* Man. Thus, it is entirely impossible that such a thing as a false Christ could exist. Hence, we perceive that an assumptive man who denied the Christ would not be anyone or anything at all. Now, let us explore the expression *the Antichrist* and see just what it does mean.

Many sincere religionists consider the Antichrist to be a universal evil spirit which is as omnipresent as is God. Now, we *know* Consciousness, God, is the Substance, Form, and Activity that comprise the entire, boundless Universe. Yet it does sometimes *appear* that a sort of universal illusory consciousness, or awareness, exists and that it is opposite to the one and *only* Consciousness which is All. In the book of Revelation, this pseudo consciousness is referred to as the "beast coming up out of the earth" (Rev. 13:11). Well, you will recall that Adam was supposed to have been formed out of the dust of the ground. And the symbolism certainly reveals all there is to the so-called Antichrist.

Adam, of course, symbolizes supposedly created, born, man with "breath in his nostrils." This assumptive man could not be explained or accounted for at all, according to our Bible:

> Cease ye from man, whose breath is in his nostrils: for wherein is he to be accounted of? (Isa. 2:22).

If this fictitious man were genuine, he would of necessity be temporary. Hence, eternal Life could never have been promised to supposedly born man. Now, this fallacious, temporary, born, or created, man would have to be opposite of, opposed to, the genuine, eternal, and *only* Man, who is the Christ. But God, being Man, is the Christ, and this Christ-Man can no more be born or created than God can be born or created. So it is exceedingly clear that it appears that there are two existences, one that is eternal, birthless, deathless, and the other being temporary, created, or born. Just as surely as there is *one* God, so it is that there is truly but *one* Man, and this Man is the Christ.

Where does this leave an assumptive, temporary man? Nowhere at all. There is no such man! Where does this leave any mind, or man, that is opposed to the Christ? Nowhere at all. There is no such mind, nor is there really any opposition to this Christ. Nonetheless, we have to face the fact that if there *were* such a thing as the Antichrist, supposedly born man would have to be this Antichrist.

There can be no such thing as a universal, omnipresent mind-man who opposes, thus is opposite to, God. This boundless Universe consists of God and of nothing else or other than God. God, being all, can only be *God*. This universal Intelligence, Consciousness, Life, Love, would certainly not exist in and as a consciousness that opposed itself. Infinite Intelligence *acts* intelligently, and it would not be intelligent for Mind to oppose Itself.

The boundless, universal Intelligence which is God does exist and manifests Itself as the Christ-Consciousness. This Christ-Consciousness is God manifested in and *as* Man. So the *only* Man there is has to be the Christ-Man, and the Christ-Man does not oppose himself. Rather, he *knows* himself to *be* the Christ. The Christ-Mind, or Intelligence, does not oppose or deny Itself. The Christ-Man is genuine. He exists as the very manifestation of what God is, only that which God is, and all that God is. This is the Father being the Son and the Son being the Father.

It is utterly impossible that such a fallacy as a false Christ could exist. If there were such a thing as a born man, he would not even know there was a Christ-Consciousness. How could he pretend to be something that he knows nothing of at all? That kind of non-man could know nothing because he would *be* nothing. In order to exist, Man has to know that he exists. In order for Man to know that he exists, he must be conscious, and this means that he must be aware as the Consciousness that knows what he *is*. Thus, the only man that exists is aware as the

Christ-Consciousness, aware *as* what It is, all that It is, and *only* that Christ-Consciousness which It is.

God manifested is the Christ-Man. The Christ-Man is God fulfilling Its purpose by manifesting, evidencing, Itself as what God is; God manifesting Itself—not to save so-called sinners and certainly not to heal man's so-called diseases. If there were such things as disease, inharmony, trouble, sin, etc., God would have to be the disease, the sin, the trouble, the sinner, and all that is completely opposite to that which is God. In short, God would have to be both the imperfection and the one who is imperfect. This, of course, is ridiculous. God can only be God.

The one indivisible Christ-Consciousness is not separated into many separate consciousnesses. Although the Identity forever remains the same, the infinite Christ-Consciousness is never divided into separate consciousnesses called men. Beloved, herein is our Oneness. This God, being Love, never opposes Itself. It just goes on being Love. The Christ never opposes Itself. So there truly is no Antichrist because there is no anti-Love.

Light and Love,
Marie S. Watts

November 1969

In the beginning was the Word, and the Word was with God, and the Word was God.
—John 1:1

Dear One,

It is wonderful receiving your letters expressing such gratitude for the glorious Truths you are seeing, thus, being. More and more of you are consciously experiencing being the absolute, eternal, constant Perfection that you are, that you have always been, and that you everlastingly will be.

The gratitude you experience is the only true and genuine Thanksgiving. As the Thanksgiving season approaches, it is only natural that our attention should be specifically focalized on the significance of gratitude which, of course, *is* Thanksgiving. Yet our gratitude is never giving of thanks for something we have received or even hope to receive. Neither do we "count our blessings" and give thanks for blessings received. Actually, we know that we can neither receive nor give anything. But we are grateful, and this gratitude is indeed a joyous experience.

Yes, we are grateful, and this gratitude represents itself as being humbly awed because we are permitted to truly *see*—thus *be*—the glory that is our Being and the Being that is everyone and everything. Perhaps it would be well at this season to again read some of the articles published in previous November issues of *The Word*.

Once again, the bush outside my study is laden with bright red berries. Oh, the Beauty of the berries, interwoven with the lush green of the foliage, is so beautiful. We have never known this bush to be so teeming with berries as it is now. Thus, we know that the feast, which is

Supply, for the migrating birds will guide many birds to the bush. Always we marvel at the infinite Intelligence and Love that manifests Itself as the berries and as the birds, who know where and when to come for necessary food. No doubt this year they will remain with us for many days.

The Beauty that is God is so evident here. The roses are in full bloom, and there is glorious color everywhere. And there are no words to describe the glory of the sunsets. No two are alike, yet it is the same Beauty manifesting Itself, and manifesting Itself everywhere constantly and infinitely. Wherever we are, this Beauty has to be, for *we* are the Beauty Itself.

Self-revelation Versus Reasoning

Beloved, as you know, you are completely free to read, study, and contemplate the writings of the Ultimate in any way that feels right to you. Nonetheless, it is increasingly apparent that some recommendations be stated that will be most helpful in your study of these writings. Always, I have refrained from giving advice or presenting a "method" for your study and contemplation. So you will realize the following statements are not in the nature of advice, nor are they the presentation of a method. Rather, they simply state the meaning of *full-open Consciousness* and the reason why it is so essential to a full and complete Self-revelation of the significance of the Truth behind and beyond the words. As you know, the words merely symbolize the Absolute Truth.

Always before and during our class experience, I have stated the necessity to be full-open Consciousness. Repeatedly it has been emphasized that all revelation is—indeed must be—Self-revelation. No one can reveal the Absolute Truth to someone whom he considers to be another. Any attempt to do so would be dualism. Identity is an absolute Truth, and the Identities that comprise Infinitude are innumerable. Yet there is *one indivisible Consciousness, and there is no separate or "other" Consciousness to whom this glorious Truth can be revealed.* This is the reason *all* revelation has to be Self-revelation, and Self-revelation can only be experienced when there is conscious, full-open Consciousness.

Sometimes someone will ask, "What is full-open Consciousness, and how do I attain it?"

Beloved, this boundless, unlimited Consciousness can never be *attained.* It must be perceived through Self-revelation. You see, *you are full-open Consciousness.* But it is impossible for this boundless openness to be Self-revealed so long as a suppositional born mind is cluttering up the premises, and whenever we are trying to understand, interpret, analyze, or reason out the meaning of the words we read or hear, this is exactly what is taking place.

Most of us have experienced Self-revelation as full-open Consciousness. Perhaps we have not realized it at the moment. Even in our days of our study of metaphysics, we may have experienced Self-revelation without being fully aware of the tremendous significance of the event. For instance, it is possible that after reading some words of Truth, we may have suddenly realized the Absolute Truth behind and beyond the words. Perhaps we were not even consciously considering the Truth when the revelation was experienced. We may have been driving, carrying on a conversation, or even washing dishes, when the Light would suddenly break. We may not even have associated the revelation with anything we had been reading. Yet later on, when we were again reading some statements of Truth, we would suddenly exclaim, "Oh, so *that* is the real meaning of those words." Often we have read the words over and over, without perceiving their full significance. But when we least expect it—when we are not trying to think—the glorious Truth behind and beyond the words asserts Itself. Then we know, and we know that we know.

Often someone will report that an entire page of one of the writings will suddenly be illumined. Once, in New York City, when we were experiencing that which we called a class, someone suddenly burst out with the following statement, "Oh, I must tell you that almost always when I read *The Word*, the pages will suddenly become a blazing Light. Yet the letters stand out sharply against this background of Light." What takes place when these events are experienced? The Consciousness of the one reading the words is full-open, and there is no attempt to interpret or analyze the words.

When we view the beauty of the rose, a sunset, or a sunrise, we do not try to analyze the reason why they are so beautiful. Neither do we try to interpret the meaning of such beauty. We are simply viewing, as full-open Consciousness, the Beauty that is revealing *Itself*. Absolute Truth has the Power to reveal Itself and needs no help from "man with breath in his nostrils." Always it is the assumptive little born "I" that tries to analyze the words that merely represent Absolute Truth—and it won't work.

At one time, I studied metaphysical literature with a dictionary at hand, and all I ever gained was more twoness, or duality. It wasn't enough. Then I turned to questioning, silently listening for the answers to be revealed. This obviously was a necessary step, but it was not until I realized that it is only because the answer *is* that the question can even occur, that I perceived the necessity to be full-open Consciousness. Then, as full-open Consciousness, it was revealed that *I am the answer to any question that could ever be asked.*

Then, too, Self-revelation pointed up the fact that if a question seems paramount in my Consciousness, it really means I already *know* the answer. So I make no mental effort to discover that which I already know. Why do I know the answer? Because *I am the answer*. You see, You, I, Everyone exists as the very Presence of every Absolute Truth. Thus, we exist *as* the full and complete answer to any seeming question or problem, and when we know— really *know*—our Self, we are aware of *being* all the answers there are.

Now, of course, we do not read statements of Absolute Truth as though we were reading a fairy tale or a work of fiction. We read *attentively* but effortlessly. Always we are aware that only because we *are* this completeness that is all Truth do we know whatever Absolute Truth is being symbolized by the words. There is an awareness that *this is the way it is*. We know we are full-open Consciousness, fully aware of perceiving and being every Absolute Truth that could ever be presented or symbolized in any way.

If the statements in any of our writings seem difficult to understand, it is simply that we are trying to understand, to analyze, the meaning of the words. Should this seem to be the case, it is better to put the book aside for a while. Many of you are finding it helpful to return to the book *Just be Your Self* and the book *The Ultimate,* in order that just the basic statements of Truth may again be perceived. As the revelations are more and more completely presented, it is more imperative to be positive that we are reading the words as full-open Consciousness.

This fact has become increasingly apparent, as the writings have followed one after another as ever increasing Self-revelatory Light. For instance, the second volume of the 1968 classnotes, *The Ultimate Awareness, an Eternal Constant*, should never be studied or discussed in a group. It is far better to read these classnotes in the silence and the full-openness that is only possible when we are in privacy. Certainly, there shouldn't be any group discussion *about* these writings. All that happens is that many so-called human opinions will be voiced, each one positive that he or she is right. Self-revelation is never experienced in this way.

Beloved, all the writings of the Ultimate are the Light revealing Itself. Not one word of these writings has anything to do with a so-called thinking or reasoning (non) mind. Of course there is no effort to "think" what should be written or typed. There isn't even questioning about what should be presented. It is all contemplative, silent listening, and as the words come, they are typed.

These Absolute Truths can only be revealed as your experience the same as they were revealed as mine. You see, there *is* one Consciousness, and the Consciousness you are, as I am and Everyone is, is truly revealing Itself this moment. The revelations I experience are your Self-revelations, and the Self-revelations you experience are my Self-revelations. So, beloved One, let us be forever free from trying to learn that which we already know and to be or become that which we already are.

Light and Love,
Marie S. Watts

December 1969

*In the beginning was the Word, and the Word was
with God, and the Word was God.*
                                           —*John 1:1*

Dear One,

Now I must thank you for all your wonderful and
loving Christmas greetings. I marvel at the Beauty and the
Love evidenced by these expressions of living Light. The
Christmas season is always such a joyous occasion. This
is particularly true for those of us who *know* that Jesus was
never born, never came into being, and thus, never could
have died or gone out of being. The very same Christ who
walked and talked with the disciples and the multitudes
consciously exists this day and every day throughout beginningless, endless eternity. So of course, we do not com-
memorate a so-called birth date for this birthless, deathless
One called Jesus. But it is a season in which unselfed Love
is manifest perhaps more generally, and the evidence of
this infinite Love is exceedingly apparent.

We rejoice in the knowledge that the ever-present,
eternal Christ-Consciousness is present in, through, and as
every one of us. In this sense, every day and every moment
is the Now which signifies Christmas for us. Then, of
course, we have a day which is called New Year's Day.
Well, of course, there is great significance behind this
holiday also. It helps us to remind our Self that Newness
is an ever-present, eternal, constant Fact, or Truth, and *we
are the Truth that is constant Newness.* Newness is not
something that comes and goes. Rather, it is equally present
as the eternal Now of our existence. It is in the awareness

of this fact that we rejoice, not alone on New Year's Day, but constantly and eternally.

The Constancy of the Presence

What a wonderful and glorious thing it is to be aware of the constant Presence of God. This means, of course, that God is omnipresent as what God *is*, all that God *is*, and *only* that which God *is*. Knowing that the very word *God* signifies the I AM that is the entirety of our Being, we are conscious of being this Presence because there is nothing else, or other, for us to be. Therefore, we are never absent from God because we can never be absent from our God-Self, or God being our Self.

In Jeremiah 23:23-24 we read:

Am I a God at hand, saith the Lord, and not a God afar off? Can any hide himself in secret places that I shall not see him? saith the Lord. Do not I fill heaven and earth? saith the Lord.

In speaking of God, Jeremiah could just as well have asked, "Am I a God afar off, and not a God at hand?" Indeed so. In the Infinity that is this Universe, there is no time, nor is there any space. The constant Presence of the All is complete, total, entire, equally present infinitely and eternally, and this Allness knows no lapse from being and from being Itself.

Sometimes we will hear someone say, "I called upon God, and He heard my plea and answered me." Then again we hear, "I reached out to God." Such statements as the foregoing always imply a God who is "afar off" or absent from the one who appeals for help. There are many similar statements to be found in our Bible, and of course, this is dualism. There is no such thing as God *and* the Identity who is simply God being, God manifesting, yes, even God visibilizing Itself as just what God *is*. Hence, we can no more be separate from, or other than, God than we can be separate from, or other than, our Self.

Although it is true that many dualistic statements of supposed separation from God are found in our Bible, there are many statements of Absolute Truth, indivisible Oneness, also to be found in both the Old and the New Testaments. For instance, in my favorite Psalm, 139:7-12, we find David joyously exclaiming:

> Whither shall I go from thy Spirit? or whither shall I flee from thy presence? If I ascend up into heaven, thou art there: if I make my bed in hell, behold, thou art there.
>
> If I take the wings of the morning, and dwell in the uttermost parts of the sea; Even there shall thy hand lead me, and thy right hand shall hold me.
>
> If I say, Surely the darkness shall cover me; even the night shall be light about me. Yea, the darkness hideth not from thee; the darkness and the light are both alike to thee.

Isn't this a glorious statement of the constant Presence that is God being everywhere—yes, even of God being *the* Everywhere?

In John 10:30, we find Jesus saying, "I and my Father are one." Isaiah 65:24 reveals a beautiful assurance of the constancy of the Presence: "And it shall come to pass, that before they call, I will answer; and while they are yet speaking, I will hear." And in Romans 8:38-39, we find Paul assuring us of the constant Presence of God, being the Christ-Love ever present:

> For I am persuaded, that neither death, nor life, nor angels, nor principalities, nor powers, nor things present, nor things to come, nor height, nor depth, nor any other creature, shall be able to separate us from the love of God, which is in Christ Jesus our Lord.

How glorious and wonderful it is to realize the constant Presence of God. Above all is the sheer Joy, Peace, and comfort of our awareness of actually *being* this constant Presence. I have known many so-called miracles to be experienced through contemplation of the Absolute Truths which are expressed in just these few verses in our beloved Bible. Sometimes I feel it would be well to compile a list of some of these wonderful statements found in our Bible and to refer to them occasionally.

You will discover that your list will grow, as certain passages from the Bible are suddenly seen to be Absolute Truths. True it is that the wording of these statements may seem to be dualistic and orthodox, but Self-revelation often clarifies the genuine Absolute Truths behind and beyond the words.

Indeed, nothing can separate us from the constant Presence of God being our own Christ-Self. Throughout that wonderful book, *The Gospel According to Thomas*, Jesus certainly makes this fact clear. Wherever we are, whatever may be our activity, it is God who exists, and it is God who acts. Oh, it seems so easy to appear to forget the constant Presence of God being all there is of us. So often we apparently find ourselves falsely imagining that we are someone as a little separate self and that we are doing or being something other than God. In all our seeing, the first necessity is to clearly perceive the Omnipresence, the Omniaction, the Omnilove that is God, and God being *All there is of anyone and anything.*

Jesus knew, and knows, so well that of himself he could be nothing, nor could he perform any activity. "If I bear witness of myself, my witness is not true" (John 5:31). In John 14:6-10, he plainly told the disciples that it was not a separate identity called Jesus who existed and who performed the marvelous works, but that it was God who was the Presence, the Identity, and the Activity:

> I am the way, the truth, and the life: no man cometh unto the Father, but by me. If ye had known me, ye

should have known my Father also: and from hence-
forth ye know him, and have seen him.

Philip saith unto him, Lord, shew us the Father,
and it sufficeth us. Jesus saith unto him, Have I been
so long time with you, and yet hast thou not known
me, Philip? He that hath seen me hath seen the Father;
and how sayest thou then, Shew us the Father?

Believest thou not that I am in the Father, and the
Father in me? the words that I speak unto you I speak
not of myself: but the Father that dwelleth in me, he
doeth the works.

Yes, it is true that God, the constant Presence, does
dwell, live, and act in, through, and *as* the Christ. And it
is this very same constant Presence that lives, moves, and
manifests Its God-Self in, through, and *as* every one of us.
Therefore, when we see, really see, anyone, we are truly
seeing God, the eternal, constant Presence. But if we imagine we are seeing a temporary born human being, subject
to all the vicissitudes of a temporary existence, we are not
really seeing anything or anyone at all.

Paul must have clearly perceived the fallacy of man's
attempt to be something or do something of himself. In
Philippians 2:13, he says, "For it is God that worketh in
you both to will and to do of his own good pleasure."
Indeed, it *is* God who lives and acts as the I AM that You
are. It is a joyous and satisfying activity, and this God I
AM activity always fulfills Its purpose as *All that is active
in and as your entire Experience.*

Even though you may seem to be unaware of *being*
this constant Presence which is called God, the constant
Presence *is* here. If this were not true, you could have no
awareness of anything at all. Thus, you would be nonexistent. It may be months or even years in which an
acknowledgement of this Presence does not take place.
Yet It is here all the while. It has to be present because It
is always where you are, and always It is *what* you are.

Often, when I seem to be exceedingly busy, I will stop for just a few moments and softly say, "God, God, God." Then such a glorious realization of peace and Love always surges and flows in, through, and as the Consciousness that I am. This frequent acknowledgement of the constant Presence is often experienced throughout the day and night. It is wonderful to know that no matter where I am aware of being or what my activity may be at the moment, this constant Presence was—and is—all there is, all that has ever been or will ever be, of the *I* that I am.

Beloved One, all that I am, You are, even as all that You are, I am. Herein is our eternal, uninterrupted Oneness. And of course, this constant Oneness is Love Itself. Despite any appearance of a world of nations and men who are divided and who oppose, resist, and war with each other, we know that the inseparable Oneness of all Existence is an Absolute Truth. Our knowing and *being* this Truth is the Light of the world. Light is a Universal Constant, and there is no darkness at all. So let us stand in and as the constant, inseparable Oneness that we eternally are.

Light and Love,
Marie S. Watts

January 1970

In the beginning was the Word, and the Word was with God, and the Word was God.

—John 1:1

Dear One,

Now we are well into that which is called the "new year." How wonderful it is to know that we never really experienced an "old year." We are aware of the fact that whatever we were, we *are*, and whatever we will be, we *are*. Furthermore, it is all *now*, for eternity is never divided into separate periods of nonexistent time.

Oh, it is true, we have to say "yesterday," "today," or "tomorrow," as well as, "this year," "last year," or "next year." Yet all the while, we know these words are only figures of speech, or symbols, that really depict the eternity that is *now*. Therefore, we do not look forward to what the new year is to bring; neither do we look backward at something we supposedly experienced during that which is called "last year." We do not hope for a better experience this year than we experienced last year. Rather, we know that no matter what may seem to appear or to have appeared, God, Absolute Perfection, is all that we have known or been.

Beloved One, this fact is why we never look back at a seeming problem that has been supposedly solved; nor do we look forward to the solution of some apparent problem that is yet to be solved. All forever *is*, and is perfect, for All is eternally, constantly Absolute Perfection.

Always, the works of the Ultimate —Absolute Truth —are glowing more and more brilliantly as the Consciousness of all of us reveals Itself as the Light Itself. We never cling to anything in *any* way. It is only that the Light shines in ever more brilliant and constant intensity, and *we are the Light that forever shines*.

There Are No Levels of Consciousness

Often we hear someone say, "He (or she) really is a very high Consciousness." Again we may hear, "Oh, what can you expect, he (or she) really is not very high in Consciousness, you know." At first one might wonder just what could be wrong with statements such as the foregoing. But let us consider some of the fallacies represented by these statements.

First of all, they are dualistic. They imply that Consciousness is two and not *One*. Furthermore, it connotes degrees of Light, of Consciousness, and of Intelligence, or Mind. You see, if there could be one Identity who was exceedingly enlightened and another Identity who was only a little enlightened, we might just as well say that God was the complete Light as one Identity but only a little Light as a supposed other and separate Identity. This simply is not true. Truly, there *is* One alone, and there is not another.

Consciousness is neither higher nor lower. There is no such thing as degrees of Consciousness. Rather, Consciousness is complete as Itself, constantly and eternally, as that which is called Substance, Life, Activity, Mind, Intelligence, and Love. We do not say that anyone is any more or any less conscious. But Consciousness and Mind, Intelligence, are one inseparable *Isness*. Thus, since no one exists who is only partially conscious, we must realize that no one exists who is not complete Mind, or Intelligence.

Intelligence is Consciousness, even as Consciousness is Intelligence. If anyone could be only partly intelligent or partially conscious, this one would also have to be only partially alive. This is true because Life, Mind, Consciousness are all one inseparable, omnipresent, constant Existence, or Being. Of course, there could be no Life, Mind, or Consciousness if there were no Love. It is Love that *is* one inseparable *One* or Oneness. Thus, there can be no such thing as partial Love. Rather, Love is absolute, complete Love. So now we realize that we are not conscious by degrees, nor are we intelligent by degrees. We are not alive by degrees, nor do we love but partially.

There is no such thing as being a high Consciousness or a low consciousness. Right here the words *All, Completeness*, are important. Suppose, for instance, you were asked to help one who was considered to be mentally deficient. Would you say, "Oh, he is only partially intelligent, but I can help him to become more intelligent"? Of course not. Your very first realization would be that there is but one Intelligence—the indivisible, universal, complete Mind. You would contemplate along this way until you were keenly aware of the fact that every Identity in existence *is* this *complete* Mind, or Intelligence. You would also experience the great revelation that there cannot be, and are not, *any* exceptions to this complete Intelligence. Presently— oh so naturally—you would experience that great surge of Love, of Joy, and you would just be conscious that All is well because All has always been well. Above all, you would do *no* mental work in order to make complete Intelligence become more complete.

Now, of course, obviously it does appear that Intelligence may seem to be more manifest as certain Identities than as so-called other Identities. But we do know that there are not separate Identities. Right here it is imperative that we know what kind of Intelligence we are considering. Since there is but *one* Intelligence, we must be considering this *one* omnipotent, complete Intelligence. So no matter how it may *appear*, the fact we are considering is the Presence of this one complete Intelligence. Thus, we pay absolutely no attention to a nonexistent, supposed born mind. There is no such mind anyway, so why pay attention to nothing. Rather, our contemplation is entirely an awareness of the marvelous, constant Existent that is complete, universal, omnipresent Mind, Intelligence, God.

It is only in the completely fallacious, born sense of things that it appears there are levels or gradations of Consciousness. Full illumination always reveals the glorious Universe in which there is no "otherness," no inequality, and above all, no separation of the one infinite All, which, of course, is God.

There are many who speak and write of the fourth dimension, the fifth dimension, etc. Yet it is known that this is not a dimensional Universe. God, the only Consciousness there is, does not exist as dimensions of Itself. The one and only Consciousness is eternally, constantly indivisible and complete, and this Completeness precludes any possibility of an unequal or incomplete consciousness. You see, this ever complete Consciousness is equally present as Completeness in and as every iota of Its Being.

This, Beloved, is why we should never look up to anyone, nor should we look down at anyone. To do so is to deny the complete Oneness that we are. It is in the Self-revelation of *being* this Oneness that all seeming problems are perceived to be completely nonexistent. This, Beloved, is illumination, and it proves itself to be a very practical revelation in and as your daily living experience. You see, there are not two existences, one the so-called human being *and* another called the spiritual and divine Being. There is no unreal *and* real existence. It is all One, and *You* are that *One*.

In order to present just how beautifully this Oneness proves Itself to be an ever-present, practical, and daily experience, I am going to share with you an excerpt from a letter received just a few days ago. I know the writer will not object to my sharing her illumined experience with you.

She is one who has studied and contemplated this Absolute Truth for what the world would call years. One day in illumination, the inseparable Nature of all Existence was revealed. She said:

> This October, during a quiet moment, I experienced an unexpected period of illumination. The room glowed with a soft white light, and in that moment the seemingly great separation of intellect and emotion disappeared. I knew and felt the truth of the Oneness of all Being. Many experiences since then amply bear out the reality I experienced. I now can feel and act as One. Isn't it wonderful!

Indeed so. It truly is wonderful. Now there is no twoness, no otherness, no problems. Now there are no levels of Consciousness, and there are no dimensions. All is One, One is All, and despite any fallacious appearance of twoness, this Oneness is where you are because It is what you are. Furthermore, it does not require any nonexistent nonsense called time in order that that which you be, you consciously *be*.

Yes, you are the Completeness, the Wholeness, the infinite, inseparable Oneness—here, now, infinitely, constantly, and eternally. You are this non-dimensional Oneness. Always you have been, always you will be. Here and now you *are* One. Behold, there is no other for you to be.

Light and Love,
Marie S. Watts

75

February 1970

In the beginning was the Word, and the Word was with God, and the Word was God.

—John 1:1

Dear One,

Spring seems to have arrived here in Vista. We have been experiencing some very heavy rains, and the hills and valleys are beautifully verdant. It is a joy to look upon the various shades of green. Most of our trees and shrubs are the evergreen variety, so of course, we do have the beautiful and varicolored green all during the winter. But soon our roses will be blooming again, and of course, this is always the greatest joy. The birds are back again, and we are enjoying their joyous songs. One meadowlark perches on the television antenna and just pours out his Joy in song. So we can see and hear the glorious Beauty that is ever-present.

The glory is that we know it is all God, and God in ever-perfect, effortless action. It is wonderful to know that God—infinite, eternal, intelligent, conscious Life—does fulfill Its purpose by *being* Its own activity and Its own Substance in action. Joy surges and flows as we write this message to you. But above all, the Infinitude that all of us really are surges and flows constantly. Thus it is, and thus it will ever be.

The Miracle Is an Ever-Present Fact

So often we hear someone speak of a miracle as though it were something that had to *happen*. For instance, we will hear, "Oh, I wish a miracle would happen." Well, first of all, a miracle does not *happen*. Let us now explore or investigate just what constitutes that which is called a miracle.

In Webster's Dictionary, the word *miracle* is defined in the following way: "An event or effect in the physical world beyond or out of the ordinary course of things, deviating from the known laws of nature, or transcending our knowledge of these laws."

Truly the foregoing is a wonderful definition of this word. You will note that Webster does not speak of a miracle as being something supernatural. Rather, he mentions the fact that this experience is just something that is generally beyond the knowledge we seem to have at the moment. And this is true.

Actually, the miracle is ever-present. The absolute Perfection which suddenly reveals Itself, either as substance, activity, or as some wonderful protection or something of that sort, is something that constantly exists. Our difficulty has been that we did not seem to know it or to be aware of its existence. Perfection and perfect harmony do not come and go. Only that which already exists can ever be manifested. If absolute Perfection and harmony did not already exist, there could never be a sudden manifestation of this Fact. It is because absolute Perfection and complete harmony do exist that they can, and do, suddenly become manifested. Incidentally, it is interesting to note that Mr. Webster mentions the fact that a miracle is an event which deviates from the *known* laws of nature or transcends our *knowledge* of these laws.

It is never an absence of absolute Perfection and harmony that is manifested. Such so-called imperfect or inharmonious conditions have absolutely no basis in fact. They are not universal facts; thus, they cannot possibly be manifested or visibly focalized. As stated before, anything has to exist before it can be manifested.

This is an absolutely perfect Universe. Its activity is always purposeful, and It fulfills Its purpose constantly everywhere. Every day the physicists are discovering that nature, as they call it, is far more intelligent and conscious than has been ordinarily believed. For instance, just recently a physicist discovered the fact that flowers are indeed intelligent and that they recognize certain ones who enter the room where they are placed. But these sincere physicists are due to discover that all true laws of Nature are Facts and not so-called human laws. Furthermore, they are universal, omnipresent, eternal, constant Facts, or Truths. When we speak of the laws of nature, we really mean the entire Universal Principle—absolute, constant Perfection —in action. This Principle *is* every Fact, or Truth, in existence, and the activity of this Principle is the intelligent fulfillment of Its purpose.

It is not important what one may call this Principle. Of course, as far as I am concerned, it is God, and as you know, to me *God* is the most precious word in the English language. This is true because when I have spoken this one three-letter word, I know that I have named Everything and Everyone in existence. This fact is the reason for the basic premise of the Ultimate—namely, God is All, All is God. But for those of you who object to this word *God*, any word that means *All* to you should be sufficient.

But let us now return to our word *miracle*. Actually, when it is said that a miracle has taken place, all that has happened is that the natural, normal, absolute Perfection that does exist suddenly becomes visible or experienceable, or it is when some definite Fact, or Principle, of Infinity is apparent. That which is called a miracle is normal, and when some experience takes place which seems miraculous, that is normal. In other words, absolute Perfection is normal, and seeming imperfection is abnormal and not according to the Facts of Nature at all.

We have been so accustomed to hearing about seeming imperfection that it really appears that assumed imperfection is normal and Perfection is abnormal. For instance, our first greeting upon meeting a friend is apt to be, "Well, how are you?" or, "How are you feeling today?" Right here is the implication that perhaps our friend may not be absolutely perfect or aware of being perfectly harmonious.

Beloved One, let us no longer believe the fallacious evidence of imperfection or inharmony. This false inclination is not limited to our planet Earth, either. Often we hear people speak of stars leaving their original orbit and shooting through the heavens. We also hear of stars or planets crashing together; or it may be mentioned that a certain section of a star may break off and go willy-nilly on its way. Well, it also seems that on this planet Earth things get completely out of hand and that wars, hatred, riots, etc., occur. Yet we *know* that these things simply cannot be, when God—absolute Universal Perfection—is present here. And *God is All that is present here*.

So where does all of this inharmony and seeming imperfection take place? *It doesn't*. This is the fact to realize. For that matter, where does a nightmare take place? Does it really happen, and if so, where does it happen and to whom? We know the answers to these questions. So let us perceive the absolute fallacy of every so-called imperfect or inharmonious event.

This does not mean we close our eyes and pretend these things do not *seem* to be. But it does mean that we consider these fallacies to be in the realm of hallucinations or nightmares, where they belong. Only in this way are we able to be of help to this seemingly troubled world. We simply face the *appearance* of trouble or imperfection and clearly perceive the absolute Perfection that is here and that *is* going on, instead of the nightmarish appearance that pretends to be taking place. We cannot be persuaded that such a thing as evil can possibly take place or be taking place. We know that God—Absolute Perfection—*is all there is here* and that this means *Everything, every Event, Everyone, has to be God, in order to be.* It is this same way in which we view the *apparent* inharmonious happenings in the heavens, knowing all the while that they are not what they seem to be at all.

Sometimes the following question is asked: "How do we know that this is a perfect Universe?" Well, those of us who really feel that the Ultimate is the Truth also are convinced that God really is *All* and that *All*—Everything and Everyone—consists of God. We cannot even consider an imperfect God. And since God really is All, this entire Universe really has to consist of God and *only God.* Occasionally, someone will ask, "How do we know God is perfect?" The answer to this question is simple. God is Love and Love is God. There could be no imperfect Love, for Love is Perfection Itself.

Beloved, truly God *is* Love and Love *is* God. Love, God, is the only Presence or Power. God, being Love, could not possibly permit sickness, pain, hatred, accidents, riots, wars, or any of these terrible nightmares that *appear* to be taking place. So let us stand on the absolute Truth that God really *is* Love and that Love really *is* God. This, dear One, is the miracle. The ever *active* Presence of perfect Love is the ever-present, ever active Presence of infinite, omnipresent, omnipotent, perfect Love. We know that if *any* imperfection or inharmony could possibly exist at any moment, God Itself would have to be the imperfection and the inharmony. But we also know this to be impossible. So no matter how bad something may seem to be, we stand firmly and persistently in the full and complete knowledge that all is absolute Perfection and *All* is acting in and as perfect harmony.

The Bible says that if we make our bed in hell, behold, God is right there. This being true, it could not possibly be hell. Therefore, that which may seem to be hell really *is* heaven. Furthermore, we read in our precious Bible, "The darkness and the light are both alike to thee" (Ps. 139:12). Yes, this is true because the seeming darkness, rightly seen, or perceived, really *is* the Light. It is in the knowledge and awareness of this fact that the miracle, which was always present, is seen, felt, and experienced. Glory be—the so-called miracles are merely *the things that are, evidencing the absolute Perfection and Harmony that forever is.*

Light and Love,
Marie S. Watts

The Word

1970–71

March 1970

*In the beginning was the Word, and the Word was
with God, and the Word was God.*

—John 1:1

Dear One,

It is true that our great nation does seem to be in the throes of violence, ignorance, and hatred. But those of us who know the Fact of all Existence realize that such a situation is impossible. So we stand in complete serenity and in gratitude that the Light is ever more apparent and that the *seeming* darkness only signifies the Presence of the Light.

Constantly I am reminded of that beautiful verse in Psalms 139: "If I say, surely the darkness shall cover me, even the night shall be light about me." Then again, in this same Psalm we read, "The darkness and the light are both alike to thee." Yes, this is true. The one infinite, supreme Intelligence does know Itself to be the Light, and this Light is the *only* Mind that exists to know anything. Furthermore, this supreme and only Mind, Intelligence, can know *only* the Light that It is.

The spring days are indescribably beautiful here in Vista. Our family of birds has increased tremendously since the February issue of *The Word* was prepared. This increase is not only in the number of birds, but also in the variety of these wonderfully joyous and free Beings. Their glorious songs literally fill the air, and it is very much as though we were almost constantly hearing a celestial symphony. Of course, the mockingbirds and the meadowlarks are still with us, and often the mockingbirds sing throughout the night. So always there is music. It is interesting to note that the songs are always paeans of Joy, and we know they are not aware of trouble, violence, hatred, worry, and the like. Rather, they go right on singing their glorious songs of Joy. Isn't it wonderful!

Some of you have written asking how to "work" in order to bring peace to our nation and to the world. Beloved Ones, we can never bring peace *to* the world. If it were possible to do mental work night and day, it would never bring peace to this planet Earth. Our necessity is to see this planet Earth *as It is right now and as It always has been and always will be*. So long as we continue to try to change *seeming* evil into good or darkness into Light, we are going to continue to believe that darkness, so-called evil, is here now, and the *apparent* nowness of this nightmarish picture is going to appear to be genuine.

Now, there may be some who say, "But I have to do something. We just can't let things go on as they are now." Beloved Ones, there are many who are trying to do something to improve the world or bring peace where chaos seems to be. That which is called history reveals that seeming cruelty and bestiality have *appeared* to be present all through the ages, and always there have been well-meaning individuals and organizations which have tried to do something to change this horrendous picture. Their efforts failed, even though their motive was laudable.

It is only a short step from trying to actively do something as an assumptive human being and trying to do something mentally to help. Neither way works. This reveals the fact that neither way is the answer to the apparent problem. But there is a way, and this way is the effortless perception, awareness, of the planet Earth and this wonderful nation *as it is* and to refuse to be deceived by any appearance of that which is not. So we stand and stand and stand firmly in and as the constant awareness that this right here and now *is* the Kingdom, Consciousness, of Heaven, or the very Presence of God. When this glorious fact is clearly and constantly perceived, the evidence of this perception is discovered to be right here.

Beloved One, this current issue of *The Word* marks the eleventh and last year in which it will be published. It has indeed been a wonderful and joyous fulfillment of purpose. Yet I am sure its purpose will be completely fulfilled during this year of its publication. Many, many letters have come in telling of help, revelation, and inspiration through the study and contemplation of *The Word*, and I am indeed grateful it has proved to be so helpful. Even so, I realize so very clearly that it has never been the words of this publication that have brought such great revelation and so-called healing. Rather, I know that the words have only fulfilled their purpose by seemingly opening the door of the Consciousness of the Identity and reminding him or her of the glorious Truths which he or she has always known. Therefore, dear One, you will always realize that you are not dependent upon words for your full awareness of all that you are and *only* that which you are. Yes, you are grateful for the words, but you are fully aware that the revelation is always your own Self revealing Itself to Itself, *as* Itself.

The Fallacy of Condemnation

First of all, I want to say that in the July 1966 issue of *The Word* there is an article entitled "No Condemnation." It might be helpful to also read this article. [The article can be found at the end of this chapter—Ed.]

If we are to accept or believe the daily reports in the news, it would certainly seem that there is much to condemn, and of course, we hear this condemnation on every side. True it is that we do not hide our heads in the sand and just pretend that, if we don't look, the whole picture and those who seem to be painting the picture will go away. It won't happen that way.

Some frankly admit that these abnormal situations and the so-called people who are responsible for them do seem to exist and to be active in this way. We walk right up to the false picture, facing it every step of the way, but we do not see the fallacious picture. Rather, we are actually seeing the Kingdom of Heaven, and thus, we see right through the *appearance* and clearly perceive the absolute peace and Perfection that are here and that is all there has ever been or will ever be here. The ever Now of the Presence of the Allness which is God precludes the possibility of anything or anyone existing here or anywhere who is not God Being. So we are completely unmoved and undeceived by the appearance. Only in this way can we be completely free from condemnation.

Of course, as far as we are concerned, we *know* there is just one infinite, omnipresent, indivisible Consciousness, and we are that Presence. We know there really is no other or otherness. As stated in *Three Essential Steps*, "Your Consciousness is your Universe." Therefore, the entire Universe *is* the Consciousness we are. So if we do imagine that we are condemning another, we deceive ourselves. There *is* no "other" to condemn. For this reason, any so-called condemnation would have to be self-condemnation.

But where and who is the consciousness that condemns? Is there a Mind, Intelligence, other than God who can even know about anything to condemn? Is there a Presence other than God that can be aware of anyone or anything other than Its infinite, eternal, perfect, omnipresent Self? No! No! So, beloved One, we can clearly perceive that now it is necessary to go all the way in our seeing. If we even *seem* to waver or be deceived at all by this horrendous *appearance*, we are not really seeing or being the Absolute Truth, which is *all* there is for us to see or be.

Therefore, we are alert. We are steadfast in our perception of *things as they are*.

In our Bible we read:

> Ye are all the children of light, and the children of the day: we are not of the night, nor of darkness (1 Thess. 5:5).

This is true. When we fully accept the Absolute Truth, we do not accept the darkness of duality.

In this precious book, we also read that we *are* the light of the world. Yes, we are the Light that shines right where the darkness seems to be; thus, we know there is no darkness at all. We do not try to change darkness into Light; rather, we just go right on, seeing and being the Light that does exist.

If apparent duality could be measured, one might say that it is more dualistic to attempt to single out or separate a specific Identity and to condemn this one. Just now, I am reminded of the woman who was brought before Jesus and accused of adultery. This episode points up so clearly the fact that condemnation of any specific one, falsely called "another," is really Self-condemnation. This is true because there is *only one* indivisible Consciousness, and if condemnation could be genuine at all, it would have to be this one infinite, inseparable Consciousness condemning Itself. Thus, we would have a Self-condemnatory God. *Impossible*.

You will recall that after the mob brought this charge and insisted upon stoning the adulterous woman, Jesus said:

> He that is without sin among you, let him cast the first stone at her (John 8:7).

The mob, convicted by their own consciousness, slunk away. Then Jesus asked the woman:

> Hath no man condemned thee? She said, No man, Lord. Jesus said unto her, Neither do I condemn thee: go, and sin no more (John 8:10-11).

The Love that was, and is, Jesus well knew the folly of condemnation. So, lovingly he said, "There is therefore now no condemnation to them which are in Christ Jesus." This means those who know they are the Christ.

Paul also was aware of the Self-condemnation which is the only condemnation (if such existed). He said:

> Therefore thou art inexcusable, O man, whosoever thou art that judgest: for wherein thou judgest another, thou condemnest thyself; for thou that judgest doeth the same things (Rom. 2:1).

Of course, we realize that *any* seeming condemnation is entirely mythical and illusory because there is but one Mind, one Consciousness, and this one infinite, omnipresent, intelligent Consciousness can know nothing unlike, or other than, Itself. This Consciousness cannot know condemnation or anything to condemn. The Consciousness that is Light can never be an awareness of darkness. If there were such a thing as condemnation, it could only be an incomplete awareness of the Light and of being the Light. If there could possibly be anything or anyone in this world to be condemned, it could be explained in the following verse from John:

> And this is the condemnation, that light is come into the world, and men loved darkness rather than light, because their deeds were evil (John 3:19).

Yes, it does seem that supposedly born man prefers to go his way in and as darkness rather than to go all the way in seeing and being the Light, which is the Absolute. But even this apparent tendency is naught because actually there is no such man.

Light and Love,
Marie S. Watts

Excerpt
(From *The Word 1966–1967*, July)

No Condemnation

It has been said that it is far more difficult to forgive the self than it is to forgive another. The following definition of the word *forgive* is found in *Webster's Unabridged Dictionary*: "To cease to feel resentment against, on account of wrong committed."

Many sincere students of Truth have completely transcended the fallacy of holding resentment toward anyone. As students of the Ultimate, we know that the one called "another" is conscious *as* the one indivisible Consciousness that *we* are. We know that Mind is never divided into separate minds, Life is never divided into separate lives, and Love is never divided into separate loves. Thus, we perceive that any resentment we might even *seem* to hold would be resentment against the One Self.

Right here, let it be understood that we are fully cognizant of the fact that actually there *is* no mind that holds resentment. Neither is there a consciousness that is aware of anything that should be forgiven. Although as yet it seems necessary to write or to speak as though there were minds other than the One—God—Mind, we are always aware that God *is* All, All *is* God. With this basic Truth firmly established in and as Consciousness, let us proceed in our perception of the fallacy of resentment.

If there could be resentment, there would have to be something or someone separate from the Self to resent. Furthermore, resentment and condemnation are inseparable illusions. If one seems to resent or to condemn another, he or she is indulging in self-condemnation. This is true because, as clearly stated in *Three Essential Steps*, "Our

Consciousness is our Universe." Thus, any forgiveness would have to be self-forgiveness, and this would mean a cessation of self-condemnation.

The Bible states that there is no condemnation for those who love God. This statement reveals a tremendous Truth. There is no condemnation of another, for there is no other to condemn. There really is no Self-condemnation because the genuine and only Self knows nothing to condemn or to be condemned. Nonetheless, self-condemnation does seem to be very tenacious, and it can also seem to bring about unhappiness or even the accompanying illusion of bodily difficulty. No purpose is ever fulfilled by self-condemnation. Indulging in this false sense of guilt and self-hatred only makes the so-called wrong appear to be more real, and for this reason, there is apt to be a repetition of the very "wrong" for which one is condemning himself.

Any practitioner or consultant knows the futility of self-condemnation. Again and again, we have heard someone flay himself or herself unmercifully, and so long as this fallacious self-punishment continues, we have seen a continuance, in one way or another, of the very thing for which the so-called patient condemns himself. We have seen the *appearance* of illness and unhappiness continue so long as self-condemnation seems to be indulged. But above all, we have also seen Joy and Perfection evidenced at once when the so-called patient realized complete freedom from self-condemnation.

All supposed self-condemnation is duality. It has its basis in the illusion that man has a mind, consciousness, life separated from, and other than, God. Once it is clearly perceived that the genuine and *only* Identity is the Infinite Identity evidencing Itself, the illusion of self-condemnation is transcended. It is realized that this Identity is "of purer eyes than to behold evil." It is clear that the one and *only*

Mind knows nothing of evil, and above all, it is realized that we are this living, conscious Mind to whom evil is unknown.

If it were possible for your eternal Identity to be born, begin, it would also be possible for you to have experienced a past in which you made mistakes, or sinned. But the fallacy of birth implies time, and there is no time. Perceiving the eternal Identity that you genuinely are, you must perceive the changeless Nature of your Identity. Never, in the eternity of your Being, were you other than the Identity you are right now. That which you eternally and infinitely know—Pure Perfection—you know right here and right now. That which you eternally and infinitely *are*—Pure Perfection—you are, right here and right now.

You are not dual. There are not two of you. There is not one of you who is "of purer eyes than to behold evil" and a second you who is aware of nonexistent evil. There is not one of you who was born, who began, and another one of you who is eternal, There is not one of you who has a human memory of so-called past mistakes and another one of you who has, and is, the Mind to whom mistakes are eternally unknown. There is not one of you who is subject to and governed by the fictitious laws of "man with breath in his nostrils" and another one of you who is eternally and constantly the very Principle of all Existence. Thus, you are the Principle which *is* all law.

All that you have ever been, you are right now. All that you will ever be, you are right now. The eternal You exists right now. The infinite You exists right now and here. There is neither time nor space. There is only here and now. Jesus was—and is—well aware of the eternal, infinite, constant Nature of his Being. He knew—and knows—that God *is* All and All *is* God. Let that Mind *be* which was, and is, in Christ Jesus. It already is the Mind that you are. Just let It be. Never can you *become* this

Christ-Mind which you already are. Never can you *become* that which you eternally and infinitely *are*.

Beloved, when you know, really know, the pure, eternal, continuous Perfection that you are, you will also know that this perfect You is constant. Never has there been an interruption in the pure Perfection that you are. Here and now, you are completely free from all so-called memories of a past in which it seemed you made mistakes. Here and now, you are the pure, Absolute, perfect, conscious, living Mind, and you have no awareness of so-called evil desires or intentions. Right here and now, you are the Light in which there is no darkness at all. Right here and now, you live and move and have your entire Existence in, and *as*, the Kingdom—Consciousness —that is God being conscious. This is why you are eternally "of purer eyes than to behold evil." What God is, You are. What You are, God is. Thus it is, and thus it eternally remains, for Eternity is now and Infinity is here. You are that Mind to whom evil, under any guise or disguise, is completely unknown.

April 1970

In the beginning was the Word, and the Word was with God, and the Word was God.
—John 1:1

Dear One,

Thank you for your many letters expressing such great gratitude for the writings of the Ultimate. Truly, Life is a beautiful Existence when we really know the everlasting, constant, joyous, free, perfect Nature that is all Existence.

Spring is very evident right now. The roses are blooming, and it is all so beautiful. The constant newness of Life that we know everlastingly exists is gloriously evidencing Itself. Isn't it wonderful to realize that the roses do not find it necessary to make any effort in order to bloom, nor do the trees strain in order that the fresh green leaves be evident? It is no wonder that our Bible says, "Consider the lilies how they grow: they toil not, they spin not; and yet I say unto you, that Solomon in all his glory was not arrayed like one of these" (Luke 12:27).

So often, in watching the ever moving Beauty of the sunset or the sunrise, these words are vividly true in, and as, the Consciousness that I am. It is all so *effortless*. When we consider the turning of the Earth planet on its axis, its orbiting around the sun, and orbiting in and as its spaceless, timeless galaxy, I marvel and rejoice at the effortless nature of all this tremendous activity. Then I wonder why it seems that we imagine we must struggle, strain, or even toil in order to know what we are and to *be* that glorious Absolute Perfection which we have always been, are *now*, and will forever be. Of course, the timeless, spaceless Nature of all Being precludes the possibility of a past or a future. Well we know that *now* is the omnipresent Existence all there is in existence, and there is no past to remember and regret; neither is there a future about which we need be uncertain.

Recently a letter arrived from an enlightened and grateful student of this Absolute Truth, and he so beautifully stated a revelation which he experienced while reading the classnotes entitled *The Ultimate Awareness, an Eternal Constant*. I know he will be happy to share his revelation with you, so I shall take the liberty of sending it along. It is so clear and purposeful that it will be inspiring to many of you:

> As I write, it flashes in: the Ultimate awareness *is* an eternal Constant, and I realize that I have been thinking that the Ultimate awareness, an eternal, must *become* so—as if "I," by studying, meditating, or however, could make It so when It already *is*. That's the way revelation comes, when least expected, to bring alive the statement (found in the writings of the Ultimate) "Self-revelation is not experienced so long as we make an effort or try to bring it to pass."

Right here is a wonderful and clear statement of the only way in which Self-revelation can be experienced. Yes, we read, we contemplate that which we read—without effort—the same way we contemplate the Beauty of a rose. Then suddenly, when we are not even expecting the experience at all, the revelation is experienced. Then we *know*, and we *know* that we know. But best of all is the fact that we realize we *are* the Absolute Truth that we know. Thus it is, and thus it constantly, eternally remains.

Principle Versus Law

Many and varied are the laws that are supposed to govern all that exists, or appears to exist, in this world of appearance. We hear and read about the so-called laws of nature, the laws of physics, the law of cause and effect, and of countless laws that are supposed to be inescapable and all-powerful. Yet we have many times seen, known, and experienced the fact that these so-called laws can be, and have been, transcended. Every time a so-called miracle is experienced, these assumptive laws of nature are proved to be fallacious. Even a so-called healing of some supposed minor ailment, without medicines or medical help, is said to be contrary to the laws of nature. Yet we know that these things take place every day.

The spurious laws that man "with breath in his nostrils" accepts and believes pretend that everything and everyone must begin and end. It seems inconceivable to this assumptive man that anything or anyone could possibly be eternal, beginningless, and endless. Even the stars and planets are supposed to begin and end. This illusion explains why this mistaken view *appears* to be so to the physicists, the astronomers, and the most learned of our scientific men. Nonetheless, every star, every planet, etc., eternally exists, and it is only because it does exist that so-called man can even seem to discover it, to see it, and to attempt to analyze it.

We look at the tree, and it appears to have sprung from a seed or from a root system. It also is supposed to live for a certain number of years, to change, age, and die. Yet when we truly *see* this tree, we are fully aware of the fact that it consists of eternal, beginningless, endless, changeless Substance in Form, and it never began, nor can it change and end.

It is only because this eternal tree really does exist that it can appear to the supposed vision of assumptive man. It is in this same way that a star or planet is seen or discovered by supposedly born man. It appears to have begun, and it is considered inevitable that it must end, or die. Yet it is only because the eternal, beginningless, endless star or planet does exist that so-called born man can seem to see it or to discover it.

This Universe is eternally, constantly complete, and *this completeness means that every star and planet necessary to its completeness is as constant and as eternal as is the Universe Itself.* Illumination reveals the eternal, constant, ever complete Universe in all of Its Perfection, glory, and Beauty. This fact, beloved One, reveals the complete fallacy of so-called laws made and believed by assumptive man. One of great spiritual Vision said, "Man sees what he believes, and believes what he sees." This certainly *appears* to be true of this entire world as it appears to be.

Anything or anyone who seems to begin must also seem to end. Anything or anyone who seems to begin and end must also seem to be subject to the so-called laws of sickness, pain, age, decrepitude, and all the inharmony and trouble which constitute supposedly born man's experience. You see, these so-called natural laws are only "man-decreed beliefs." They can only *seem* to be true, genuine, inescapable, or powerful if we believe them and invest them with power. But when we know—*oh, when we know that which genuinely does exist*—these fictitious so-called laws hold no terror for us. We simply realize that they are only the fantasies of a *kind* of man that does not even exist.

We do not ignore them; neither do we honor them, as though they were really laws or were really invested with power. Certain it is that we do no mental work in an effort to rise above them or overcome them. Knowing that we are ever free from any such fantasies, we just go right on seeing things as they *are*, and we let the phantasmal pictures dissolve themselves. What have they to do with us? Nothing—*nothing at all.* Often we are reminded of Paul's enlightened statement:

> For the law of the Spirit of life in Christ Jesus hath made me free from the law of sin and death (Rom. 8:2).

The law of life mentioned by Paul is not really a law at all. Actually, this "life in Christ Jesus" is the eternal, beginningless, constant, endless, changeless Principle which is God, being the Christ, and *we are the very presence of this Principle, this life which is the Christ*. We are forever actively engaged in *being* this Principle in action. We are eternally, constantly Self-governed. We are not alive as a so-called born, human, temporary life, governed by assumptive laws of supposedly born man, as though we were controlled by laws outside of, or other than, our own Christ-Principle.

Principle is forever Its own Government. Principle is always perfect. Principle is eternally, constantly Absolute Perfection. We know that to be Absolute Perfection means to be absolutely perfect, without a flaw, free from impurity of any kind, without a blemish or the slightest defect. Principle cannot, and does not, vary. It can never be any more or any less Absolute Perfection than It eternally, constantly *is*.

Now let us again consider the stars, the planets, trees, etc., that were discussed earlier in this article. When, in illumination, we see and are aware of the eternal, changeless, perfect tree, star, planet, we are seeing—perceiving—beyond the seeming temporary substance and activity in form that is *supposed* to be the tree, the star, or the planet. We are seeing beyond anything that seems to have beginning, change, or ending. We are completely free from all so-called manmade laws or beliefs. A belief without a believer is impossible, and since the *only* Man in existence knows *only* that which God—the Christ—knows, there simply is no man existing who believes such fallacious, deceptive, hideous laws. Yes, that which we see, or perceive, in illumination really *is* the eternal, constant, perfect, flawless, undeviating Principle.

We are fully aware of the fact that this Principle is not a static, fluctuating, inactive existent. Rather, we are aware that It is an ever active Substance, and Its activity is always absolutely perfect activity. Principle can never make mistakes, and neither can Principle act against Itself. It stands everlastingly and constantly as the boundless, infinite, conscious, ever active, living Intelligence to which inharmony, trouble, sickness, pain must ever be unknown. But this is not all. This same omnipresent, constant, eternal Principle knows no interruption. It can never be interrupted by birth, change, or death. It knows Itself to be complete as Infinity and Eternity, and It can never know aught that is other than Its ever perfect Self.

Beloved, now you can see how absurd it would be for us to bow down to assumptive laws of a supposedly born man. Now it's clear that it is only necessary to fully accept and to honor with "all our heart, our Being, our Life, and Intelligence," *the one and only Presence, the one and only Power.* We know that to bow down to so-called laws or nonentities called born men is to bow down and to worship idols. To abide by or to fear these illusory laws is to honor them, and to honor such spurious laws is to dishonor God. So we refuse to be subservient to these assumptive laws. No matter how real, convincing, or forbidding seeming imperfection or inharmony may appear to be, we stand and stand and stand, constantly in and as our awareness of Being and *seeing only that which is Principle.*

Light and Love,
Marie S. Watts

May 1970

*In the beginning was the Word, and the Word was
with God, and the Word was God.*

—*John 1:1*

Dear One,

Our Hearts truly sing and surge in joyous acknowledgement of the glory that is God being, and God being every One and every Thing. Isn't it a marvelous thing when we experience the Presence and experience *being* the Presence? Indeed so!

In a letter recently received, an enlightened one brought out an important point. Since it is important to her, it must also be important to all of us. It had to do with our reading of the words in which this Absolute Truth is symbolized. She mentioned that often I have emphasized the fact that it is not well—indeed, it is futile—to attempt to analyze, interpret, or reason out the meaning behind the words in which Absolute Truth is symbolized. I have stated that these writings should be read as full open Consciousness and in the same awareness we experience being when we are gazing at a beautiful scene, a sunset, a sunrise, etc.

The loving writer of the letter felt that her former experience in reading as full open Consciousness must also be the experience of many sincere ones. It seems that she was specifically referring to the reading and study of *The Word.* Apparently, to her, to read as one would "when gazing at a beautiful scene, a sunset, a sunrise, etc.," meant a sort of surface reading. She brought forth some good points, and we shall now see what is revealed on these points.

To read as full open Consciousness means to read as a completely attentive Awareness. This is true because

Consciousness *is* Awareness. Now, to read, completely aware of the spiritual significance presented in the contents of *The Word* or of any Absolute literature, requires the complete, full, conscious attention to that which we are reading. It should be an all-absorbing openness of Consciousness. Certain it is that there is no dreamy drifting around, as a cloud drifts across the sky, in the study of the Ultimate; our conscious, full attention is necessary. But this does not mean that we, through any so-called mental effort, attempt to understand the spiritual significance of that which we are reading. We do not attempt to reason, we do not interpret, and we do not analyze. But we do devote our full attention to that which we are reading.

The writer of the above mentioned letter spoke of the tremendous value of reading the article in each issue of *The Word* several times. This is certainly true. Even though some of the words in which it is written may be words we have read before, we find that reading an article several times reveals more of the Absolute Truth revealed between and behind the words in which it is symbolized.

As most of you know, since 1965, when we condensed the contents of *The Word*, this Absolute Truth has come through in brief, succinct statements. Oh, beloved One, there are literally countless revelations to be experienced, and that *are* being experienced, by being "full open" but *attentive* as we read these brief statements. *The Word* does present a glorious opportunity for Self-revelation. So often it seems there are too many words used in an effort to *explain* this Truth. It sometimes appears to cover or conceal the glory that always lies between, behind, and far beyond the words in which this Truth is symbolized. Therefore, it is our sincere hope that the reading of *The Word* will be a glorious fulfillment of purpose in and as the experience of every one of you. To this end it is revealed, and to this end it is fulfilling its purpose. Great Joy surges and flows as the reports come in, telling again and again of the fulfillment of an infinite purpose through this glorious revelation.

The Spiritual Significance of Mount Zion

Our Bible is a most precious book. It has been called the "Book of Life," and thus it is, when the genuine significance is revealed of many of its passages. There are some who seem to have an antipathy for this great book; there are some who consider it to be just history; and again, we find those who ridicule and revile this important message for all of us.

Many books have been written and countless sermons preached in an attempt to interpret the Bible. This effort to interpret has only seemed to conceal the actual importance of this book and to distort the true meaning of some of its most important revelations. Any attempt to interpret the Scriptures must of necessity miss the mark because an attempt to do so involves a so-called born thinking and reasoning process.

The Absolute Truth that is *All* Existence can never be perceived by any assumed, born, thinking or reasoning mind. *There really is no such mind.* Therefore, the Absolute Truth that is so abundantly stated throughout our Bible has to be revealed. And of course, all revelation is Self-revelation. Thus, we read as full open Consciousness, fully aware of every Truth presented in this great book. We know that every Truth presented in our Bible is already present and *known*, in and as the infinite, conscious Intelligence that we are. Never do we attempt to interpret. Rather, we wait for that which we already know to announce and reveal itself as our own God-Consciousness.

Just now it seems that some references pertaining to Mount Zion are important. Our planet Earth *seems* to be in the throes of hatred, wars, crimes, sorrows, and all sorts of inharmonies. Many there are who are convinced that nuclear warfare will soon destroy all of us. If we are not constantly alert, we seem to be caught up in these fears and doleful predictions, and of course, we could then be serving no purpose at all in helping to alleviate these seeming threats and fears. Truly, in these days, we must realize that we *are* the Light and let the Light that we are shine and shine and shine. This is infinite Love in action.

There are many references to Mount Zion in our Bible. Some of them point clearly to the fact that Mount Zion symbolizes the very heights of Consciousness. For instance:

> Out of Zion, the perfection of beauty, God hath shined (Ps. 50:2).

Yes, it is only when we are fully aware of being the everlasting, eternal, Light that we clearly and completely realize the Absolute Truth, God, which is constant Perfection. It is this Light that lights the world. But it is—indeed, it *has* to be—a constant Light. It can never be an intermittent existent. Its ever-present Constancy is Its Power. Thus, there can be no break, no interruption, in Its ceaseless continuity.

This ever shining Light reveals the glorious "perfection of beauty" and the Beauty that is Absolute Perfection. This planet Earth could not be absolutely perfect if the Universe, God, were not perfect. But we must also realize that *the Universe, God, could not be perfect if this planet Earth were imperfect.* Certain it is that Absolute Perfection has to be consciously realized as *All* Existence if we are to constantly maintain the Consciousness that we exist in and as the Light. Therefore, it is necessary to stand and stand and stand, in and as the height of the Consciousness that we are. It matters not how things may appear or how insistent or persistent they may pretend to be; we do not "come down" from our Mount Zion, the heights of the Consciousness that we are, for one tiny moment in the eternity of our Being.

Of course, the suggestion may sometimes occur that we are not doing anything to help in this period of an appearance of world strife and crisis. But nothing could be further from the Truth. Actually, we are not *doing* anything from the standpoint of world opinion. But by remaining at the heights of Consciousness, we are *being* the *only* Power. It is the *being* of this Power that obliterates the seeming discord and reveals the ever perfect harmony, Love, and Peace that *is* right here all the while.

> The Lord shall send the rod of thy strength out of Zion: rule thou in the midst of thine enemies (Ps. 110:2).

If there were enemies, duality—twoness—would certainly be the most formidable of them. It is this false sense of twoness that appears to divide those called men and nations. But right in the midst of seeming hatred, strife, etc., there is the strength, the Omnipotence, that is God, governing Himself, or Itself, as all Existence. This, Beloved, is the power of our knowing.

It has been said that war is hell, and if war were genuine, it certainly would be hell. But the Psalmist sang, "If I make my bed in hell, behold, thou art there" (Ps. 139:8). God, being *the* Everywhere, means that heaven is the Everywhere, so even that which seems to be hell, truly is heaven. Our only necessity is to see it, and to continue to see it, despite an appearance to the contrary.

> Beautiful for situation, the joy of the whole earth, is mount Zion, on the sides of the north, the city of the great King. God is known in her palaces for a refuge (Ps. 48:2-3).

Yes, right in the midst of seeming turmoil, the glory that is God is All, and this glorious Love, Peace, and Absolute Perfection is all that does, or can, exist.

> The wolf also shall dwell with the lamb, and the leopard shall lie down with the kid; and the calf and the young lion and the fatling together; and a little child shall lead them. They shall not hurt nor destroy in all my holy mountain: for the earth shall be full of the knowledge of the Lord, as the waters cover the sea (Isa. 11:6, 9).

Indeed, the foregoing quotation is no prophecy. Rather, it is the way all things *are* right here and now, for *this is the Kingdom of Heaven.* Standing constantly at the very height of our Consciousness, Mount Zion, it is God —the *I* that I am, that everyone *is*—seeing and being *only* the Absolute Perfection, the eternal, constant peace, harmony, and Love that abound in and as this Kingdom of God. Thus it is, and thus we know it to be, constantly, eternally.

Light and Love,
Marie S. Watts

June 1970

*In the beginning was the Word, and the Word was
with God, and the Word was God.*

—*John 1:1*

Dear One,

Today is a glorious, all new experience, even as is
every day and night. The flowers are so beautiful, and
their perfume defies description. Oh, Life is so glorious,
so ever fresh, and so filled with the Light that is God. It is
true the picture of the world of appearance seems to be
gloomy indeed. Many there are who feel hopeless and
helpless about the world, and even our beloved Nation
seems to be torn by strife. But glory be! We are not
hopeless, nor are we at all helpless. We know that the
only world there is or could be is the *Kingdom of God* and
that heaven—complete harmony and peace—are the only
facts of Existence. But best of all, we know our perception of this Truth is purposeful and that it does fulfill its
purpose.

If assumptive man, with all his efforts and organizations, could have brought peace to the world, all that is
called war would have ceased long ago. Organizations for
ending all wars have been going on for a long while. Yes,
even wars have been fought in order to end wars. Of
course, this is only in the seeming. Yet the tragic delusion
called war seems to go right on. Consequently, we can see
that assumptive man, no matter how well intentioned he
may be, does not and cannot prevent this same non-man
from warring against himself. But we know that "earth is
but heaven when rightly seen," and there are no warring
people or nations here at all. We can rejoice in the fact

that our knowing of the Truth is purposeful; it *is* powerful because it is the Truth that is already true.

The absolute Truth is always the only Fact of Existence, whether we seem aware of It or not. Herein is the power of our contemplative "knowing." Therefore, we are unmoved by *any* appearance of inharmony, no matter how horrendous or persistent it may pretend to be. "Ye are the light of the world," and the Light is inextinguishable. So we stand in the Light, as the Light. We never fluctuate and we never falter. We just *know* God is All, All Is God.

The Completeness of Each Identity

Again and again, questions arise pertaining to reincarnation. There are many sincere students of Truth who firmly believe that man is born and lives many lives in his upward climb to complete absorption into the infinite All. But these lives and deaths, if such there were, would only lead to the end of the identity itself.

Those who believe in reincarnation also believe that the identity must be born into or with a new body at each reincarnation and that he must depart from this body at the moment of supposed death. If this were true, the iden tity would have to be bodiless, or formless, before birth and again after death. But form is necessary to the completeness of *any* Identity, and an interruption of this completeness would mean an interruption in the Identity Itself. There can never be an incomplete Identity. Neither can there be Substance without form.

All Substance is Consciousness, Life, Intelligence, Love. This Substance is constant and It is eternal. The astrophysicists tell us that the Universe consists of atoms and that even the atmosphere itself is comprised of structural atoms. Having seen photos of clusters of atoms, we realize that the atom is not formless. So the very basic Essence of all Existence exists in and as form. Of course, all of the foregoing does not alter the fact that the atom itself *is* Consciousness. So we will not be confused by this symbolic terminology.

Our purpose at the moment is to perceive that the form, or body, is necessary to the completeness of any Identity. But there is another aspect of the Identity that we will now consider. This word *completeness* is of paramount importance for every one of us. However, just now, let us realize the *Completeness* that is necessary in order that the Identity really *be* consciously eternal and constant. For instance, if Life could be temporary, the Identity could not possibly be eternal. A life subject to interruption in its very existence would be an incomplete life. This is true because Life is God and God is eternal. Hence, there can be no incomplete life.

There can be no unconscious Life, nor can there be a lifeless Consciousness. Since living Consciousness in form *is* the Substance that is the Body, this Substance in form has to be eternal, constant, and eternally, constantly, consciously alive. Consequently, there can be no conscious existence without a consciousness of the Body. And consciousness *of* the Body is living, intelligent Consciousness *being* the Body. So this Body is as eternal as is the conscious Life that comprises this Body. Without a consciousness of the Body, the Consciousness Itself would be incomplete. Thus, we would have an unconscious, unalive, non-intelligent Identity. This, of course, is utterly impossible.

Let us be clear on this one point. We have no quarrel with our friends who so ardently believe in reincarnation. Surely this belief has been helpful to many identities. For one thing, it sometimes helps them to have a hope for another life to come, in which they will have another chance to do better or to be better. But of course, this very fact carries along with it the so-called law of karma, and as stated in our textbook, *The Ultimate*, we cannot believe that such a cruel law could possibly exist. You will find more on this subject of karma in the chapter entitled "No Karma" in *The Ultimate*. However, since God is the *only I*, who is the Identity that sins and that must suffer or be punished?

Of course, each one of us has to be completely free to accept or reject anything he reads or hears. Freedom is an Absolute Truth. Only in complete freedom can the Consciousness be full open for further Self-revelations. Nonetheless, Freedom is an eternal Universal Constant, as is every Truth. So we do not quarrel with anyone's right to accept and believe whatever seems right to him at the moment. Yet it seems imperative to state that so long as we remain convinced that reincarnation is a fact, we are going to continue to seem to be born and to die. Surely, since God *is* Love, there must come a day when we *know* there is neither birth nor death. *But this does not mean that we have to be devoid of our Identity in order to perceive this simple, yet profound, Absolute Truth.*

Indeed we can, and do, reach a point beyond the cruelty of so-called birth and death. We are aware of the eternal completeness of each Identity and of the fact that the Body is as eternal and constant as is the Consciousness, Soul, Life, etc. But this glorious Freedom does not seem to be perceived so long as we continue to accept an *appearance* of a temporary body as though it were ever the genuine and only Body Itself. We know there is one Body only and that we do not have or experience a temporary body and another Body that is eternal. Therefore, we accept only the beginningless, changeless, endless Body that does exist everlastingly.

When we are fully aware of the Nature of all Substance and the fact that all Substance exists in and as form, we no longer have any concern about a *kind* of body that does not even exist. We do not even need to give any undue consideration to the Body at all. In fact, at this point, it is far better to "consider the heavens, the work of his hands" than to dwell too much upon the subject of Body. But until we have reached the point of complete immunity to every seeming supposition of a born body, it is necessary in certain instances to be specific where the Body is concerned.

Of course, you realize we are not referring only to the Body of the Identity called Man. As stated before, all Substance exists in and as Form, and there is *no* Substance existing that is not in form. Hence, we are speaking of the Body of the tree, the rose, the blade of grass, a grain of sand, and even the Body of the atom Itself. It is so glorious to realize the infinite variety in which all Substance is manifested. But the ecstasy is experienced when it is perceived that, although the Substance in forms is infinite, *there is no division of this Infinite Substance at all*. The ceaseless activity of this Substance is as inseparable as is the Substance Itself.

Now the question may arise as to whether the Body of the Identity remains eternally the same Body. Indeed so, and let us perceive why it *has* to remain the same identical Body.

We have realized that the Body consists of the Consciousness, the Life, the Mind, and the Love that is the Identity. Now, this Consciousness remains the same identical Consciousness; therefore, the Body has to remain the same identical Body. The Consciousness of the Identity is eternally conscious of being the specific, but inseparable, Identity that he is. For instance, no one can be the Identity you are *for* you. Always you, and you alone, are aware of being your identical Self. Thus, in order to be eternally complete, it is necessary that you, as a specific Identity, be eternally aware of *being* the specific, eternal Body that is necessary to your completeness. Yes, the Identity is forever conscious of being Himself and Himself only. His very awareness of being Himself is His only awareness of being the Body. Consequently, the identical Body of each Identity is as constant, as continuous and eternal, as is the Identity Himself.

Finally, beloved One, the Substance that is alive here is Life eternal Itself. The Substance that is conscious here is eternal, continuous Consciousness Itself. The Substance that is intelligent here is Mind Itself. Above all, the Substance that is always perfect here is perfect Love.

Light and Love,
Marie S. Watts

July 1970

In the beginning was the Word, and the Word was with God, and the Word was God.

—*John 1:1*

Dear One,

First of all, I must thank you for your many letters of appreciation for the article entitled "The Completeness of Each Identity," which was in the June 1970 issue of *The Word*. As the Absolute Truths presented in this article were being revealed, a great surging sense of complete joy and fulfillment of purpose was intensely present. When this feeling is so pronounced, I always know that the writing is to fulfill an important purpose, and so it has proven itself again. I am so grateful.

Many of you realize that through further study and contemplation of the articles in *The Word*, the Consciousness you are does experience greater and more complete revelation. Yet you also perceive that you are not learning any Truths that are unknown to you. Rather, it is that you are simply reminding your Self of these glorious Truths that you have always known.

As you know, you could not possibly be conscious as a partial Consciousness. The fact that you are conscious at all has to mean that you are totally conscious. Therefore, the total Consciousness you are is aware of, and *as*, all Truth. Yet it does seem that we must remind ourselves of these Truths occasionally. Isn't it wonderful to realize that we are truly unlimited and boundless in our full totality and completeness in all ways! Indeed so. The further we see, or perceive, this Truth the more we realize that we are free from all limitations. Actually, the word *limitation* has no place in our vocabulary. Beloved, herein is complete freedom and joy everlasting.

Let us continue to see the world, and especially our own beloved Nation, as it *is*, rather than as it appears to be. The *only* activity that can possibly be going on is Omni-action—God in action. God, being all Intelligence, Life, Consciousness, Love, is constantly, eternally, infinitely active, and this activity *is* intelligent, loving, ever harmonious, and purposeful. Furthermore, it is peacefully and joyously fulfilling Its purpose. No matter how horrendous the false appearance may be, it is our necessity to stand firmly and continuously in and as the Light that *is*, rather than in and as the seeming darkness that *is not*. This, Beloved, is what it means to *be* the Light "that lighteth every man that cometh into the world" (John 1:9). Therefore, we stand in the Light, *as* the Light, and we know there is no darkness at all.

The Pearl of Great Price

Among the so-called ancients, pearls were considered to be the most precious of gems. No doubt this is the reason why Jesus, speaking metaphorically, compared this precious gem to the kingdom of heaven.

> Again, the kingdom of heaven is like unto a merchant man, seeking goodly pearls: Who, when he had found one pearl of great price, went and sold all that he had, and bought it (Matt. 13:45-46).

A few mornings ago, I awakened hearing the words "the pearl of great price." I knew it was to be the title of this article. Even so, I did not realize the tremendous and glorious revelations that were to be experienced as I silently contemplated these words. Indeed, the pearl of great price, or the most precious of all gems, is the Absolute Truth, and this Absolute Truth really *is* the kingdom of heaven. The word *Absolute* means complete perfection, purity, without a blemish, without a flaw. In short, it means complete harmony. And complete Absolute Perfection *is* the kingdom of heaven.

It is notable that something definite was required of the merchant in order that he obtain this pearl. He found it necessary to sell all that he had if he were to obtain this most precious gem. Of course, we know that all the money or all the so-called possessions in the world could not pay for the Absolute Truth in Its purity. We cannot weigh this glorious Truth in the balance with anything of a mercenary nature. But the revelations go much deeper than anything that has to do with so-called possessions. There certainly is something required of us in order that we perceive and experience the kingdom of heaven. Let us now perceive just what this requirement entails.

When one of the scribes asked Jesus, "Which is the first commandment of all?" Jesus clearly stated that which is required of us in order that we may perceive and be the kingdom of God, or heaven:

> And Jesus answered him, The first of all the commandments is, Hear, O Israel; The Lord our God is one Lord: And thou shalt love the Lord thy God with all thy heart, and with all thy soul, and with all thy mind, and with all thy strength: this is the first commandment. And the second is like, namely this, Thou shalt love thy neighbor as thyself. There is none other commandment greater than these (Mark 12:29-31).

The foregoing is a wonderfully complete statement of that which is required of us in order to perceive, and experience, being *in* the kingdom of heaven *as* the very kingdom itself.

First of all, it is essential for us to truly and fully perceive the basic Truth that God really *is* All, thus All—

everyone and everything—really is God. It can be no other way, for there is nothing existing but God for anyone or anything to be. Thus, the Oneness, the indivisible, infinite, omnipresent Allness that is God, is our basic premise. There can be no qualifications of this Absolute statement of Truth. We must accept and acknowledge this Truth fully and completely. But this is not all; we find that to give *any* credence whatever to something that could not be God means that the kingdom—Consciousness—of heaven, which is the entirety of our Being and Body, is not fully realized and experienced. Thus, our first requisite is to stand steadfastly on our basic premise: God is All, All is God.

Indeed, we do love God and God alone. We do love God with all our heart, our soul—Consciousness—and all our Mind, or Intelligence. But we know that we are not loving a God outside of, or other than, the God-Self that we are and that *everyone* is. Incidentally, it is only in loving in this way that we can truly know what Love is and what it means to really love. This Love is completely impersonal. Yet It is strong, ever enduring, and above all, It is completely unselfed.

Oh, there is such great power in this infinite Love. Actually, all of our seeing, all of our knowing, is null and void unless we truly feel and experience the Presence that is this Love. Only in this way can we love with all our strength. You see, Love is the fire of It. Love is the Light of It. Love is the inseparable Oneness, the Allness, that holds everyone and everything in and as complete Absolute Perfection. Thus, Love Itself *is* the kingdom of heaven.

Love is not something that is static. Rather, Love is a vibrant, living, constant, surging, flowing experience, and in order to experience this Love, *we have to be Love Itself.* It is in this way that we truly love our neighbor as our Self. We clearly perceive the glorious Truth that our neighbor is none other than our God-Self, even though our neighbor is an Identity. But this Identity can never be separate from the one infinite, conscious Love that all of us eternally are. Eternal Love is the *only* Love. It never begins, nor can It ever end. It does not come, nor can It go. It does not fluctuate. It is never interrupted, because It is a universal Constant. It is ever perfect because perfect Love is the *only* Love there is or can ever be.

Beloved, in all the seeming turmoil, it is necessary for us to be constantly alert. To accept duality at all is to open wide the door to all sorts of delusions. In a world that seems to be rampant with so-called hatred, strife, injustice, etc., it is no small matter to stand firmly and constantly in and as this Absolute Truth. And when it appears that *we* are troubled, it requires great steadfastness for us to just refuse to accept or believe the seeming arguments of inharmony.

This is particularly true if something seems to say it is painful or a threat to our Life. But right here is where we do stand. We are adamant in our refusal to be moved from our constant knowledge that all *is* Absolute Perfection and there is none else. We refuse to have any "other gods." We refuse to acknowledge or to believe *any* fallacious evidence of imperfection. We know that to do so would be to dishonor God. We know that any deviation from the basic premise—the Allness, the Oneness, that is God—means a denial of the Absolute Truth that God truly *is* All. No matter how things may appear, we ask, "Is this God?" If it is, then it is—and *has* to be—Absolute Perfection. If it appears to be imperfect or inharmonious, it only *appears* to be—but actually it *is not*. We know that all Being is God-Being, and God is always being God. There is nothing else or other for God to be but just God.

Thus, completely free from all duality, we find that we truly are existing in and as the "holy of Holies." We know that we are in the kingdom of heaven, *as* the kingdom of heaven Itself.

> And the twelve gates were twelve pearls; every several gate was of one pearl: and the street of the city was pure gold, as it were transparent glass (Rev. 21:21).

Yes, Beloved, we do live and move and have our Being in and as the Kingdom of God—here, now, constantly, and eternally. Let us *stand*.

Light and Love,
Marie S. Watts

August 1970

In the beginning was the Word, and the Word was with God, and the Word was God.

—John 1:1

Dear One,

Beloved, the month of August is rapidly approaching its close, and of course, it has for several years been our custom each year to have our class experience at some period during the month of August. It has been beautifully interesting to note your response to the fact that this year we would dispense with our usual classes, seminars, etc. It is true that some of you have seemed to feel bereft, at least for a while. But it is also true that some of you have inherently felt the rightness of the revelation that no class in the Ultimate was to be experienced this August.

From the depths of my Heart, I have hoped this period would mean a tremendous surge of Self-revelation as the Consciousness of all of you. I am so very sure that ultimately *all Revelation has to be Self-Revelation*, and when we realize the Truth of this fact, we no longer feel the need to search further for any greater awareness of the Absolute Truth. No longer do we search for teachers, masters, or whatever, in an effort to gain more understanding of the beautiful Truth we are, that we always have been and will eternally *be*.

Does this mean we are never again to attend classes, study the works of the Absolute, or listen to tapes? No! No! No! What it does mean is that our Self-revelation goes right on, whether or not we experience classes, study the Truth, or listen to tape recordings. But glory be—once we are experiencing Self-revelation, our Oneness in, and as, a class experience is literally "out of this world." Far more complete and meaningful than ever is our study and our purpose in listening to the tapes. The purpose is more beautifully fulfilled than we have dreamed to be possible. It is almost as though we had been bound by chains hitherto; suddenly the fetters of our self-forged chains simply dissolve, and we are *free*, boundless, limitless, and infinite.

This, Beloved, is the way we *really are*. Our only necessity has been, and is, to fully perceive it, accept and thus experience being, this glorious, ineffable freedom. Above all, we love—oh, how we love. Indeed, we do love because we realize *we are Love Itself*. At last we know what we are, that we have to *be* what we are, for there is naught else for us to be.

The Silence Beyond Words

So often when we are reading words that symbolize the Absolute Truth, we reach a point of Absolute silence. Then we no longer read, nor do the words on the page have any significance for us. Sometimes we will continue, for a while, to be conscious of unspoken words, but again we reach a point when we just know, and there are no words. It is at this point of infinite knowing that we are aware of being the "silence beyond words," and we know the meaning of the statement "silence is golden." We are aware of the Light and of *being* the Light. Generally, the Light is at first a glorious golden glow, and the feeling is *Love*, surging and flowing in great circular waves of tenderness. Oh, it is so wonderful, and no words could possibly describe or express it.

As we remain in this still, glorious silence, the Light may vary, or It may be seen as an indescribable white brilliance that is far brighter than the sun. (This Light could never be seen by so-called born eyes, so we do not misinterpret this "seeing" as human vision.) We may be conscious of myriads of colors and forms. Again, we may be conscious of only this Light, which we inherently know to be Life Itself. Without so-called thought or words, we *know* this Light, Life, is the *only* Life that is alive or that can be alive.

Oh, there is activity, but here again, no words can describe this activity. It has to be experienced in order to truly know that the activity is absolute stillness, and the stillness is an *active* stillness. Silently the "still small Voice" speaks, and we hear, realizing that we are the speaker, even as we are the one who hears. But there are no words spoken or heard. It is just awareness.

God is All, All is God. Now the full meaning and significance of this glorious Truth is perceived, and we are conscious of the infinite, omnipresent, omnipotent Omniaction that is eternally and inseparably One. Then we truly *know* God, and knowing God, we know the Self. Yes, we know the Self, and to know this is to know God. There is no other way.

Of course, no two experiences of illumination are exactly the same. This is not an attempt to describe this illumined experience in words. It would be futile to make any such an attempt. Yet the Power, Love, that is felt is always present. As stated in *You Are the Splendor*, there are infinite varieties of aspects of illumination and innu-merable aspects in which it can be experienced. Seeing and consciously being the Light is but one aspect of illu-mined seeing. The foregoing is but a feeble attempt to express in words the wondrous illumined experience that was going on as this article was being revealed. Actually the experience is continuing this moment, but in the aspect that is necessary to the fulfillment of this distinct purpose, that is, *The Word* revealed and evidenced.

Our Bible abounds in instances that reveal diverse aspects of illumination. Let us consider the experience of Elijah when it seemed his life was being threatened:

> And he came thither unto a cave, and lodged there; and, behold, the word of the Lord came to him, and he said unto him, What doest thou here, Elijah? …
>
> And he said, Go forth, and stand upon the mount before the Lord. And, behold, the Lord passed by, and a great and strong wind rent the mountains, and brake in pieces the rocks before the Lord; but the Lord was not in the wind: and after the wind an earthquake; but the Lord was not in the earthquake:
>
> And after the earthquake a fire; but the Lord was not in the fire; and after the fire a still small voice (1 Kings 19:9, 11-12).

It was necessary that Elijah experience this aspect of illumination. He was seemingly fleeing for his Life, and there was a purpose to be fulfilled through this experience.

Actually, when we know what illumination signifies, every illumined experience is purposeful. Many of us will recognize the experience of the "still small voice" which speaks so silently and so wordlessly. We *know* the Love, the Power of the wordless silence, and we rejoice in seeing this Power in action. The irrepressible activity is always a fulfillment of purpose. Yet, paradoxically, during the glorious experience we have no awareness of any purpose or of the fulfillment of any purpose. It is all just the experience of knowing, seeing, and above all, *being*.

David, the Psalmist, often experienced the omnipresent Infinitude which is God. Under the stars, in complete solitude, aware of the timeless, spaceless, Allness that is God, he too heard the still small voice. He saw and felt, and experienced, being the very Presence and Power of the Love that is Infinitude. The 139th Psalm, which I so often quote, is the evidence of this infinite Consciousness of things *as they are*.

Moses was in great illumination when the children of Israel were led through the Red Sea. When Moses retreated into the solitude of the mountain, the Ten Commandments were revealed. Surely he heard the still small voice. He interpreted what he heard in words, as many of us do. It is the stillness, the complete silence, that reveals the Heaven that *is*, rather than the seeming hell that is not.

There is no God in the whirlwind, the earthquake, or the fire. There is no God in hatred, strife, war, greed, etc. No! But right where all this apparent turmoil *appears* to be, there is God and God alone. You will recall that Jesus instantly stilled the seeming storm when the disciples feared they were doomed. Jesus had no awareness of any storm. His illumined Consciousness revealed the calm, the peace, the complete safety that did exist, rather than the supposed storm that did not exist.

Beloved, the winds, the earthquakes, the fires can appear to be evident in many ways. These distortions of Truth may seem to be manifested as wars, strife, hatred, bondage, dictatorships. It may appear they attempt to parade as illnesses, pains, worries, lacks, and in heartbreaks. Yet the still small voice always reveals the Kingdom of infinite, omnipresent Absolute Perfection, Peace, and Joy that is God being All, All being God. We know we can never change anything, nor can anything be healed. God is never in need of change, nor can God be in need of healing. Our only necessity is to *see all things as they are*. This is when we, in silent listening, hear the still, small voice.

Light and Love,
Marie S. Watts

September 1970

In the beginning was the Word, and the Word was with God, and the Word was God.

—John 1:1

Dear One,

Your letters are beautiful, and my Heart rejoices as I read them. Words can never express the Joy I experience when you report that you are experiencing your own glorious revelations. Truly, Self-revelation is the basic purpose of the Ultimate, and it is being fulfilled. So I must say, "Thank you" for telling me of these Self-revelatory experiences. But the simple words "thank you" can never convey the surging happiness I feel. Gratitude *is* Joy, even as Joy is gratitude.

Many of you have written or called expressing gratitude for the article in the most recent August issue of *The Word*. Some of you have reported so-called healings as the article entitled *The Silence Beyond Words* was being read and contemplated. Some of you have experienced seeing and being the Light that you are, as the Absolute Truth presented in this article was revealing Itself as your Consciousness. Oh, glory be!! I am not surprised, because the Light is ever more constantly revealing Itself. And the Love! Oh, the Love is so beautiful and so powerful that puny words seem futile in which to describe this surging, flowing experience of *being* the Light that is Love, the Love that is Light.

The Comforter

The infinite, eternal Love that was, and is, so beautifully exemplified by Jesus is forever constant. This impersonal

Love never fluctuates. Its Omnipresence is never absent. It is the Love that Jesus was and is; it is the Love that you are and that I am. Always, eternally, we have been this Love. Forever we will be this Love. It does seem that for just a little second in the eternity of our being, we may have forgotten that we *are* everlastingly this Love; we may have appeared to try to separate It into personal love or loves. But one day, we "open our eyes," and we discover this indivisible, eternal, infinite Love, and we ecstatically realize that *we are this Love.*

The words and works of Jesus the Christ are positive, practical manifestations of the fact that he knew, and knows, himself to *be* this eternal, constant Love. It was in being this Love that he fulfilled his purpose so gloriously. This he did by being visible even to so-called born eyes of assumptive man. But Jesus knew that the disciples considered him to be a master, or teacher. He also knew that ultimately the Absolute Truth would have to be Self-revealed. (In *The Gospel According to Thomas*, he clearly told Thomas that he was not their master, and he revealed just why he was not a master.) He tried to make it clear to the disciples that so long as he remained visible to them and they clung to him as a so-called personal savior, they would not really perceive the glorious, complete revelations that are Self-revealed.

But Jesus knew the disciples were sad and distraught because it was necessary that he become invisible to them. Being the Love that he was, and is, he tried to explain as best he could and to comfort them:

> And I will pray the Father, and he shall give you another Comforter, that he may abide with you forever; Even the Spirit of Truth; whom the world cannot receive, because it seeth him not, neither knoweth him: but ye know him; for he dwelleth with you, and shall be in you ... At that day ye shall know that I am in my Father, and ye in me, and I in you (John 14:16-17, 20).

> Howbeit when he, the Spirit of truth, is come, he
> will guide you into all truth: for he shall not speak of
> himself; but whatsoever he shall hear, that shall he
> speak: and he will show you things to come (John
> 16:13).

Beloved, what is the Comforter? Is it a leader, teacher, or master? Is it some particular outlined way to follow? Is it found in some organized religion? No! Jesus clearly stated that It is completely impersonal and that It is the "Spirit of truth." Where is It to be found, and how is It to be revealed? A contemplative study of the foregoing passages from John will reveal that this Spirit exists as the very Christ-Consciousness that is the Identity of every one of us. This Spirit of Truth is the entirety of our Being. This Spirit, Consciousness in form, is the Body of the Christ, or the Christ-Body of Light, which is really visible when we are truly seeing aright.

Now, how far away from the Comforter are you? Can you discover this Comforter, Christ-Consciousness, by searching or by making some mental effort? Can some teacher, leader, or master reveal the Christ-Self that you are *to* this Christ-Self?

You *know* the answers to these questions. It is Self-revelation that reveals the complete Oneness that is God being the Christ and the Christ being Man. Jesus knew this to be true, and he informed the disciples of this fact:

> At that day ye shall know that I am in my Father,
> and ye in me, and I in you (John 14:20).

He could have said, "I am the Father, and the Father is the *I* that I am. I am the Christ that you are, even as you are the Christ that I am"—and it is all God being. Oh, it is so simple. We say it every time we say, "God is All, All is God." But it seems we do not perceive the Comforter unless, or until, our Self is Self-revealed *to* the Self, *as* the Self.

126

Those who have experienced this great Light almost always ask, "Why didn't I know this before? Here I have always been just what I've known myself to be. It is all so beautifully simple."

Indeed it is simple. But somehow it seems we have insisted that we had to *do* something in order to attain this glorious perception. So we have attended lectures and classes with the objective of learning more *about* God; we have read Truth literature, trying to analyze, to reason, or to be taught something through our study. Yet all that took place was a little more knowledge *about* God or what some author or teacher believed God to be.

What does your Self-revelation that your Christ-Consciousness is the Comforter mean? What does it reveal? Beloved, first of all, it reveals your infinite, free, boundless Being. It reveals the beginningless, birthless, endless, deathless Nature of your Being. Yes, you are aware of being infinite, eternal, constant, immutable Absolute Perfection. And the Joy! Oh, the ecstasy of the complete, unconfined, unlimited *Freedom* can never be described.

When there is a conscious awareness of the Body, it is truly *the eternal, ever perfect Body*, and you know this eternal Body is the *only* Body you have ever known or experienced being. But specifically, you know that *this* eternal, perfect Body has been your *only* body throughout this whole miasmic appearance of a temporary body. It has only seemed to be obscured by a mist, a misconception without even a misconceiver. But the Comforter does reveal the glorious fact that this eternal, perfect Body *is* visible; It has always been visible, and It will always be visible. Thus, the promise of the book of Revelation is fulfilled:

> And there shall be no more death, neither sorrow, nor crying, neither shall there be any more pain: for the former things are passed away (Rev. 21:4).

This is no prophecy. Rather, this Heaven is the way things are, the way they have always been. This is the Comforter, and you can joyously say, "I am That."

Light and Love,
Marie S. Watts

October 1970

*In the beginning was the Word, and the Word was
with God, and the Word was God.*
—John 1:1

Dear One,

Oh, there is such great activity being experienced here. It is wonderful to experience the ever greater activity of the Ultimate. How grateful we are that our family, being one inseparable Consciousness, is permitted to be constantly involved in this glorious activity.

Needless to say, "my cup runneth over" with Joy. Yes, the Absolute Perfection that is, is perceived, experienced, and manifested as we read effortlessly, yet attentively, the glorious Truths that are our own Consciousness. How marvelous it is to know these Truths have always eternally existed in and *as* our Consciousness, our Being, and our eternal Body.

Now, it seems imperative that certain phases of our activity be clarified. As you know, it has seemed necessary that I remain for the most part in seclusion. This fact, coupled with many other aspects of this Self-revelatory period, has apparently been misunderstood by a few of you. Many letters come in whose writers have become convinced that I have been or am preparing to become unavailable, perhaps even invisible, to those who seem to require occasional interviews, classes, or direct communication in some way.

I am indeed happy to report that this simply is not true. The long periods of silent listening were indeed necessary. But there is most certainly a purpose to be fulfilled by this silent listening. I rejoice in the fact that it is being fulfilled and will continue to be fulfilled.

So, beloved Ones, let us go forward in, and *as*, this glorious, ever active, *eternal* Christ-Consciousness. You know, the Ultimate Absolute really is true. And being true, it can be, and is being, evidenced as the absolute, constant, eternal, perfect Life which it reveals. Let us completely erase all the old patterns which have been foisted upon us throughout the ages. Let us be full open to the glorious, ever newness of eternal, constant, living, intelligent, loving Consciousness which is forever aware of being. "Therefore if any man be in Christ, he is a new creature: old things are passed away; behold, all things are become new" (2 Cor. 5:17).

Incidentally, Love never becomes unloving. Love never withdraws or withholds Itself from those who seem to need help. Love is always conscious of being and of being present wherever and whenever it is the fulfillment of Its tender purpose in being. Love can never be absent, for Love is the ever omnipresent Christ which is God being. Thus it is, thus it has always been, and thus it will forever be.

Dear One, the article that follows is a sequel to the article entitled "The Comforter" in the previous (September) issue of *The Word*. Before you read this current article, it will be most helpful and inspiring if you would again read the above-mentioned article. Of course, you are free to read in any sequence that feels right at the moment. But my feeling is one of a vast sense of completeness being experienced as the two articles are read in sequence.

The Purpose of the Comforter

It is interesting to note that the astrophysicists are now aware of the fact that this is a purposeful Universe.

Some even have expressed surprise at the discovery of just how purposeful this Universe is. Well, it is not surprising, because all Substance, all Form, and all Activity exist as the fulfillment of a specific as well as an infinite purpose. There is not so much as one atom, blade of grass, grain of sand, etc., that is not necessary to the complete fulfillment of purpose that is this Universe. What is the Universe? What is anything and everything? God, God, God. What else or other than God is there for anyone or anything to be? Nothing, beloved One—nothing at all.

Of course, all of the foregoing is merely leading to the fact that there certainly is a purpose to be fulfilled, and that is *being* fulfilled, by the Comforter. Jesus was never deluded. Neither did he delude himself. He knew he could not be a personal savior to, or for, anyone. Yet being Love Itself, he recognized what appeared to be the need of the disciples as well as the seeming need of every one of us. Thus, he spoke of the Comforter and promised that this Comforter would reveal Itself as the Spirit of Truth.

Now, we must perceive the meaning of the Spirit of Truth. All Truth, every Truth, is an Absolute Truth. There is no such thing as a dual Truth. Absolute Truth is a Universal Constant, present everywhere, infinitely, constantly, eternally, and as you know, the word *Absolute* means absolute Perfection, free from anything other than this complete Perfection. Absolute, infinite, eternal, constant Perfection is a basic Fact of all Existence. Since we are to perceive the purpose of the Comforter, it is now essential for us to know just what this purpose is and in what way this purpose is fulfilled.

Now let us ask: what was it that enabled Jesus to "speak the word" and it was done? What was it that revealed the visible and experienceable evidence of Perfection right where seeming imperfection had appeared to be?

Oh, beloved One, Jesus the Christ was, and is, conscious only of Absolute Perfection. Being the very Presence of the Christ-Consciousness, he could only see, perceive, know, and experience the Absolute Perfection that is God. You see, the Christ-Consciousness *is* the infinite All, God, being conscious. There is no such thing as a dual God. Duality, twoness, otherness, is unknown to the infinite, conscious Oneness that is God. Being All, and being the Absolute Truth that is Absolute Perfection, God can know only what God *is*, and this means that God can only be conscious of the Absolute Perfection which is God. This Consciousness *is* the Christ-Consciousness. It was, and is, this Consciousness that perceived *only* the Absolute Perfection which is all that ever exists, right where so-called others imagined they saw and experienced imperfection.

Suppose those surrounding Jesus did appear to see a withered hand. Jesus merely said, "Stretch forth thine hand." Jesus was well aware of the way the onlookers seemed to mistakenly see this hand. But he was not deceived. He was not deluded. He knew there was a hand before him, but he saw only the hand that consisted of Absolute Perfection.

The Comforter is Self-revelation. Its purpose is to reveal the fact that Absolute Perfection is all Substance, Form, Activity. The fulfillment of the glorious purpose of the Comforter is the visible evidence of the Absolute Perfection the Comforter reveals. It is to *experience* this evidence and to see it experienced wherever we are aware of being. This fulfillment of purpose means to perceive only eternal Life where an assumed temporary life may seem to be. It means to perceive success where failure may appear to be the case. It means to perceive Joy where sadness may appear to be, peace where struggle and strife may seem to be.

Beloved, the Comforter *is* come. Always the Comforter has been. Everlastingly It will be. Jesus knew, and *knows*, this to be true. The Comforter is the eternal Christ-Consciousness, the Spirit of Absolute Truth. Every Identity *is* an eternal Identity. But to be an Identity does not mean to be a separate, or other, being than the *One All Infinite Being*—God. The eternal Identity that you are could not possibly exist unless this eternal Identity were the Christ-Consciousness. Thus, the Christ-Consciousness, or Comforter, is always eternally present as your very existence and as the Identity you are. But this is not all. Wherever the Comforter *is*—and always It is right where *you* are— Its purpose and Its fulfillment of purpose also is, and is evidenced.

Now it is my hope that you will, as full open Consciousness, turn to our beloved Bible and read the sixteenth chapter of the Book of John. Here Jesus plainly says, "I have yet many things to say unto you, but ye cannot hear them now" (John 16:12). Throughout this entire chapter, Jesus lovingly, tenderly reveals the necessity for Self-revelation, the purpose of Self-revelation, and the fulfillment of this glorious experience. He well knew that each and every Identity would ultimately discover that he is the Christ, or God, being Man.

Above all, he revealed that the day would come when no one would any longer look to a personal teacher, leader, or savior. Rather, everyone would fully perceive and be the *visible* evidence of the ever living Christ. No longer would it seem to be necessary for Jesus or anyone to appear to have become invisible. Thus shall be revealed the spiritual significance of the following statement of Absolute Truth:

And God shall wipe away all tears from their eyes; and there shall be no more death, neither sorrow,

nor crying, neither shall there be any more pain: for
the former things are passed away (Rev. 21:4).

In Light and Love,
Marie S. Watts

November 1970

In the beginning was the Word, and the Word was with God, and the Word was God.

—*John 1:1*

Dear One,

I must thank you for your many letters of appreciation for the September and October issues of *The Word*. Every day brings more reports of illumination, inspiration, and Joy through the reading and re-reading of the articles in those two issues. But that is not all; many reports of what the world calls healing have been received, and I do not believe we have ever received so many reports expressing gratitude for the writings as we are now receiving. I just felt you would like to know.

Incidentally, the articles titled "The Comforter" and "The Purpose of the Comforter" are only the nucleus of revelations too numerous and glorious to mention just now. But I can say that much more is being revealed on the Comforter. It is my earnest hope that you will continue on with those two articles and see the *glory* that is to be revealed as those revelations fulfill their purpose in and as your experience.

Thanksgiving Day will have passed before you receive this issue of *The Word*. But I know that your "Thanksgiving" is a continuous experience. I also know that you do not give thanks for so-called material things and blessings. Rather, you are unceasingly grateful just because *you know what you know, and you know that you know*. Gratitude *is* always Joy.

In any event, I know that you were happy during Thanksgiving and that you are joyous every day and

135

every night. How could it be otherwise, when you are aware of being the very Principle which is Joy? It is small wonder that our Bible says, "Come before his presence with joy." It also enjoins us to "rejoice always." Oh yes, Joy *is* a constant experience in the freedom and the fulfillment of purpose we experience as we continue on our way as the Absolute Truth, which is complete Perfection here, now, and forever.

Beloved One, there is much activity being experienced that we have not as yet mentioned. But very soon we will be able to report the details of our joyous Ultimate activity. In the meantime, I know that the Joy you *are* is infinite, constant, and eternal.

The Importance of Listening

Sometimes it seems that we make one mistake right after another. This appears to happen, no matter how good our intentions may be or how sincerely we try to "do the right thing." Then we question, "What is the matter with me? I rely wholly upon God, and I try to live this Truth." Once in a while, we find that we are just a little sorry for ourselves. (Beloved, only one who has seemed to experience just this sort of frustration can really know how puzzling it can appear to be.)

The very fact that a seeming problem is encountered means that the answer is already here and ready to reveal itself. The answer is very simple. Actually, it is so simple that, when it is revealed, we wonder why we have not been aware of it long before we appeared to have made all the mistakes.

What is the answer? *We have not waited and listened for that "still small voice," that impulsion that leaves no doubt whatever as to what course to pursue.*

To many sincere students of the Truth, it appears that God directs them if they rely wholly upon God and if they try to "live this Truth." Oh, all of us seem to have been misled by this mistaken concept. So we have to recognize that the "father of lies," *duality*, appears to have been operating—successfully—in and as our Consciousness, thus, in and as our affairs.

Now let us ask, "If God were to direct or guide us, wouldn't it mean that God was guiding *man*, someone separate from, or other than, Himself, or Itself?" Truly God *is All*. This being true, who exists other than God being to direct or to be directed? Beloved One, God, the All as All, constantly fulfills every purpose, both infinitely and specifically. The Infinite and the Specific are *one and the same God*. This being true, it is really futile, even impossible, for any one of us to act as though we were someone separate from, or other than, God. Furthermore, God is Self-directed, Self-controlled, and always Self-governed. Who and what is this infinite, but specific, Self? It is God *being* God, yet God *being* all there is of you, your affairs, your daily experience, and as your bodily affairs.

Our seeming mistake has been that, although we apparently turned *to* God, asking for guidance, we failed to "be still" and listen for the answers to our questions. We expected these answers to come from a Being who was outside of, or other than, our own Consciousness.

There is no God being other than the God who is being the I—the Identity that you are, that I am, that everyone is. Oh, beloved One, the omnipresent God, being all there is of you, does not even need to ask any questions. God, your own conscious Intelligence, Mind, always knows all there is to know. Whenever a specific fulfillment of purpose is necessary, this ever-present God, being You, knows the answer and the way in which the purpose is to be fulfilled.

Now, do we really have to *try* to live this Truth? We know that God is all Truth. Would we *try* to live God? Of course not. God, all Truth, all Life, lives as His own Truth, His own Life. There is no one other than God, Life, who can live at all. Consequently, we have no choice other than to live, or be alive as, this Truth. Always, it is the assumptive little non-existent "I" that imagines it can know anything, do anything, or be anything apart from, or other than, God. Yes, God is the All Knower and the All "Be-er."

Jesus the Christ was, and is, completely aware of this fact. He said, "I am the way, the truth, and the life: no man cometh to the Father, but by me" (John 14:6). Yes, not one of us truly perceives that he exists as *what* he is unless he is fully aware that he *is* God, being the Christ, being God. Actually, there is no one who can know anything, do anything, or be anything other than the Christ, Man, who is God *being*. Jesus made this fact exceedingly clear in many statements of absolute Truth.

Let us consider just a few of Jesus' statements that so clearly reveal this absolute Truth. For instance, in John 5:17, we read: "My Father worketh hitherto, and I work."

And in John 14:10, we find this enlightening statement:

> Believest thou not that I am in the Father, and the Father in me? the words that I speak unto you I speak not of myself: but the Father that dwelleth in me, he doeth the works.

You will realize just what Jesus meant when he spoke of God being *in* him, because he had clearly stated, "I and my Father are one." Hence, Jesus knew that he was speaking of the fact that God was living, or alive, as the one they called Jesus. This fact is the genuine meaning of the Christ.

Oh, there are so many of Jesus' statements which clearly reveal his awareness that he was, and is, just what

God is and nothing else, or other. It is interesting that Paul also at least glimpsed this glorious Truth and that it was, and is, true of all of us.

> For it is God which worketh in you both to will and to do of his good pleasure (Phil. 2:13).

Now, let us perceive just why it is so necessary to listen, really listen, for that "still small voice" until we *feel* that certain impulsion which leaves us no choice other than to act as we are impelled to act. Never do we ask for guidance as though we were seeking help from a God who is outside of, or other than, our own Consciousness. Neither do we seek enlightenment on any course of action and then rush ahead, supposedly thinking and acting as though we could do something of ourselves apart from, or other than, God being the Actor and the Activity. Rather, we silently consider the absolute Truth that because we are, and have no choice but to be, the conscious Mind, Intelligence, which is God, we are constantly, eternally aware of everything it is necessary to know for the complete fulfillment of any necessary purpose. We are conscious of being "full open." We do not make a so-called human decision, nor do we even begin to act, *until we hear the silent, or sometimes audible, words, or until we feel that certain Impulsion which leaves us no choice other than to speak or act as we are impelled to act.*

Oh, beloved One, in this way, and only in this way, can we always be sure that we cannot make any mistakes. God never makes a mistake. In fact, mistakes are unknown to the Mind, Intelligence, that is God. Our activity is God in action, and it is always successful. It can be no other, because you see, it is God who acts as our Activity.

In Light and Love,
Marie S. Watts

December 1970

In the beginning was the Word, and the Word was
with God, and the Word was God.

—John 1:1

Dear One,

Your letters are such beautiful paeans of sheer Joy that I must again thank you for these glorious expressions of Love. Yes, the Light that is revealed and experienced as Self-revelation *is* Joy and constant gladness. Life is completely free, untroubled, and the unlimited fulfillment of purpose. This experience, Beloved, is the Heaven that is, and eternally remains, our infinite yet specific abode. We are fully aware of the wonderful fact that Life truly is beautiful.

As the Christmas season approaches, the awareness of *being* unselfed Love literally floods our entire Being, and we are grateful for the many evidences of Love that we encounter wherever we go. Truly, we *know* that Love, Joy, and absolute Perfection are inseparably One, and we constantly rejoice in this beautiful Oneness. We have received many beautiful cards from you, and our Hearts are overflowing with thanks. Words are indeed poor substitutes for the Love we feel as we rejoice at the Beauty of the cards and the wonderfully inspired poems that reveal so much between and beyond the lines. So we will just say, "Thank you, thank you, thank you."

Now, as the Christmas season is here, we are exceedingly aware of all of you. We would wish all the Joy of Infinity for you, but we know that you already have, thus *are*, all that we could wish you to have. So we are just rejoicing in the certain knowledge that you are complete as Joy, as Fulfillment of Purpose, as Absolute Perfection, as *All that God is*, for the Allness that is God is *All that you are*, here, now, infinitely, eternally, So in our Hearts we sing, "Joy to the world, the Christ *is* come," and *we are That*.

The Constant Joy of Being

Yesterday morning I awakened with the following words singing in and as my Heart: "Our God is a joyous God. Our God is a happy God. Our God is mirthful and always ecstatic. Our cup runneth over with Joy, Joy, Joy."

Free from all limitations, all restrictions, all heaviness, dourness, and gloom, we rejoice always and in all our ways. In all our ways we acknowledge God and fully perceive God to be the *All*, the *Only*, the Omnipresence, the Omniaction, the Beauty, and the Glory that is *All*. Our Joy is boundless, constant, eternal, and infinite. We know that Joy is a universal, constant, omnipresent, eternal, absolute Truth. And we also know that we are this absolute Truth. We know that we are the sum total, the aggregate, of every absolute Truth. But the ecstasy of *being* Joy Itself is a constant experience.

Our Bible abounds in statements of sheer, ecstatic Joy. David, the Psalmist, gazing into the boundless heavens, sang great paeans of Joy:

> Let the heavens rejoice, and the earth be glad; let the sea roar, and the fullness thereof. Let the field be joyful, and all that is therein: then shall all the trees of the wood rejoice (Ps. 96:11-12).

Yes, Joy is unconfined. Never can Joy be limited or separated. Nor can Joy ever be any greater or lesser than the completeness that is Joy.

The Joyous Heart is forever free. This complete freedom means fear is unknown, nor is there any awareness of anything to fear or be feared. We are free from all false sense of responsibility; we are free from all judgment or condemnation. We know nothing of foreboding, worry, or burdensome depression, and we can sing with David, "The lines are fallen unto me in pleasant places; yea, I have a goodly heritage" (Ps. 16:6).

The assumed shackles of supposed human, or mortal, laws are dissolved. We live and move and have our being as the Christ, the Comforter, in whom there is no sorrow and no sadness at all. We know that Joy is an infinite, absolute Truth. Joy is omnipresent, eternal, absolute Truth. There is not one moment in Eternity and not one pinpoint in boundless Infinity in which Joy is absent. We gaze upon the leaves of the tree, literally dancing with Joy. We hold the rose cupped in our hands and feel the petals quiver in ecstasy. We listen to the birds as they sing the freedom and Beauty of their Joy. We are conscious of *being* this pure, uninhibited Joy, as the happy, playful kittens or puppies scamper joyously and freely across the floor. We hear the joyous laughter of the happy child. We sit beside the flowing stream and hear the joyous chuckling as it flows freely along.

Let us again consider another ode to Joy sung by David, the psalmist:

> Make a joyful noise unto the Lord, all the earth: make a loud noise, and rejoice, and sing praise ... Let the sea roar, and the fullness thereof ... Let the floods clap their hands: let the hills be joyful together (Ps. 98:4, 7-8).

And in Psalms 16:11, we again find David joyously singing:

> Thou wilt shew me the path of life: in thy presence is fullness of joy; at thy right hand there are pleasures forevermore.

Beloved One, we experience being the boundless Joy in the spaceless, timeless silence of the desert. We experience being this Joy in the midst of the thunder and lightning of the storm. We experience the ecstasy of just *being* Joy, wherever we are and whatever our activity may be. In the deep silence, there is the Joy of soundless laughter. In the song or the symphony, there is the glorious Joy of living, moving Beauty, called music. In the work of art—the painting, the sculpture, or whatever—there is the poetic Joy of infinite grace, Beauty, and absolute Perfection. At the seaside, the constant movement of the waves, whether boisterous or exceedingly calm, is joyous, free activity— and we know that *we are That!*

Joy and freedom are inseparably *One,* and because we are aware of *being* Freedom, the Principle Itself, we are eternally, constantly free. Thus, we are eternally, constantly joyous. Sometimes one, not quite understanding our spontaneous Joy, will question, "Why are you so mirthful? Why do you suddenly and unexpectedly break forth in laughter? Why, in the greatest moments of Self-revelation, do you suddenly laugh?"

Well, we know why we are so joyous. We know that we *are* Joy. But above all, we know what we are, what everyone is, and why all of us are just what we are. Jesus has been called the "man of sorrows." Nothing could be further from the Truth. He was, and is, constant Joy Itself. He revealed this fact to the disciples in the following words:

> These things have I spoken unto you, that my joy might remain in you, and that your joy might be full (John 15:11).

Jesus made this statement immediately after he had informed the disciples that he must go away. He knew they were sorrowful, and he also knew that sorrow does not exist in and as the Consciousness that is God being conscious. So, being Love Itself, he enjoined them to consciously be the Joy that they actually were—and are.

You will recall that Jesus had promised that the disciples would not be left comfortless but that the Comforter would appear. We rejoice constantly in the knowledge that the Comforter is present, has always been present, and will forever be present, We joyously acknowledge that the Comforter can never be separate from our own God Self Being because God, being the Christ, *is* our only Self.

We rejoice in our constant awareness that God, the All, is the *only* Presence, the *only* Power. We know—and know that we *are*—the Peace that passeth all so-called human understanding and that this very planet Earth is truly Heaven. The indivisible Oneness that is God, being everyone and everything, is the Love that we know and that we *are*. Yes, Beloved, we are in Heaven, for we *are* Heaven. Here there are no warring nations, no power-mad little born men. In all of the boundless Infinitude which is God, there is no hatred, strife, or struggle—a*nd we are That.*

> And I saw a new heaven and a new earth: for the first heaven and the first earth were passed away ... And God shall wipe away all tears from their eyes; and there shall be no more death, neither sorrow, nor crying, neither shall there be any more pain: for the former things are passed away (Rev. 21:1, 4).

Yes, the revelator saw all things as they *were* before illumined Consciousness revealed the Heaven that is Earth and the Earth that is Heaven.

Beloved, we rejoice that *now* this Heaven is our Earth; now this Earth *is* our Heaven. Infinitely, eternally, Heaven and Earth are *One*. And glory be, we are that One that is All; we are that All that is One. We love, oh, how we love, for we *are* the infinite Oneness that is Love. Thus, we rejoice constantly, infinitely, eternally.

Light and Love,
Marie S. Watts

January 1971

*In the beginning was the Word, and the Word was
with God, and the Word was God.*
—*John 1:1*

Dear One,

Thank you for your many letters of appreciation for
the article on Joy in the December issue of *The Word*.
Many of you are still writing us about the continuing Joy
and revelation through further reading and contemplation
of this particular article. Your Joy is our Joy, even as our
Joy is your Joy. Until or unless we are experiencing this
glorious, effervescent Joy, we are not really experiencing
our God-Being at all. Joy is so natural, so normal, that it
does indeed seem odd that more of us do not perceive and
constantly experience this irrepressible, bubbling Joy that
is God, being joyous.

Self-revelation reveals that there is no purposeless
activity. All activity is God, Intelligence, being active. God
is constant activity. Therefore, all activity is intelligent
activity. Intelligent activity is purposeful activity. Needless
to say, the Mind, Intelligence, that *is* the activity is also
the purpose as well as the fulfillment of the purpose of its
activity. Therefore, Beloved, every word of the Ultimate,
whether written, printed, or spoken, is purposeful. It is all
God, revealing and manifesting as the activity, as its purpose, and as the fulfillment of its glorious purpose.

Your letters and calls are the proof that this purposeful
activity is being fulfilled as your experience. Of course,
the experience *is* the Experiencer, and *you are That.* But
the important factor here is that you are experiencing Self-
revelation. Beyond all so-called teachings or teachers,

beyond all twoness, or "otherness," you stand. Full open, whole, and complete, you rejoice in your awareness that because God *is* All and All *is* God, you are—you have to be—just what God is and nothing else or other.

This, Beloved, is what Self-revelation always reveals. You can see why my Heart literally sings in greatest Joy when you write or phone telling of your own glorious, joyous Self-revelations. Thank you, more than words can say, for your reports of wonderful Self-revelations. We continue on to ever greater, more joyous, more glorious revelations and the fulfillment of purpose of these revelations. Above all, Self-revelation reveals the infinite, eternal, boundless, indivisible Oneness of all existence. This is Love Itself. *We are That.*

Self-Revelation

Again and again, we have realized that Self-revelation is imperative. We know that only through Self-revelation can we know what God *is*. Thus, only through Self-revelation can we know what *we* are. True it is that the first necessity is to realize that God really is all that does exist or can exist. It necessarily follows that all that does or can exist is, and *has* to be, God. It is only in this realization that we experience revelation. The awareness of the fact that all Existence is God being, and God being *God*, is full and complete Self-revelation.

Complete Self-revelation is beyond *all* duality, beyond all twoness, beyond all otherness, and is beyond all "seeming." It is beyond all questions about the seeming world of the seeming man with "breath in his nostrils." Often someone will ask, "Why does there even *seem* to be inharmony, war, sickness, birth, and death; why it is that everything *seems* to begin and end?" Well, so long as we continue to question as to the reason for the "seeming," we are still concerned with the appearance of otherness. This being true, there must remain some duality called the little self lurking around. Full, complete Self-revelation is not experienced so long as we are at all concerned with what is called the seeming. Rather, a constant awareness of the Allness, the Onliness, of God precludes the possibility of *any* questioning or any concern about the non-existence called the seeming.

In our beloved Bible we read:

> Thou wilt keep him in perfect peace whose mind is stayed on thee (Isa. 26:3).

To keep the mind stayed on God means to be completely unconcerned with anything or anyone that is not, and could not possibly be, God. Thus, there is no awareness of an appearance of non-existence called the "seeming." So long as the seeming is of any importance at all to us, it also is going to seem to be genuine to us, at least to some extent. But a complete awareness that "nothing" really *is* nothing means a complete Self-awareness of the Omni-Something which is *All*. Hence, there can be no awareness of the nothingness called the "seeming." Thus ends the questions pertaining to "nothing."

It is well to realize that this full, complete Self-revelation cannot be taught. It cannot even be learned. It can never be our experience through so-called mental effort, analysis, reasoning, or any so-called mental gymnastics such as yogi mind exercises. *It just won't work.* It may seem to do so for a while and to a certain point, but it never truly leads to full, complete Self-revelation. There is a point beyond all this preliminary "fencing" with Absolute Truth. The Absolute permits and admits no partials, no qualifications, and no deviations. It is necessary to go *all* the way, and to remain all the way, in our awareness of

Absolute Truth and of *being* this Absolute Truth, which is God.

Full, complete Self-revelation is the Christ, and the Christ is the full, complete revelation of the Allness, the Onliness, that is God. Revelation cannot be taught, nor can it be learned.

> It is written in the prophets, And they shall be all taught of God. Every man therefore that hath heard, and hath learned of the Father, cometh unto me (John 6:45).

Jesus well knew, and knows, the tremendous importance of these statements. Who or what does it mean to be taught of God? Well, God is the *only* Consciousness, the only Mind, Intelligence, that does exist or can exist as anyone or anything. Thus, to be taught of God means to be so conscious of the Allness, the Onliness, that is God that absolutely nothing else or other means anything or is of any importance *to* us or *for* us. Once we have fully perceived this glorious Truth, we are aware of the Christ, and above all, we are aware that we *are* the Christ. To whom could, or would, the Christ turn for teaching?

Yes, indeed, everyone who is taught of God—who experiences complete Self-revelation—"cometh unto me," or perceives that he or she *is* the Christ. Thus, we perceive that Self-revelation is the ever-present Christ that *is* Man, revealed, identified, and evidenced, and *there is no other evidence of man*. To accept, acknowledge, or believe any other evidence of Man is duality, and duality can never lead to complete full Self-revelation.

Once full, complete Self-revelation is experienced, it is as though we had come full circle. In *The Gospel According to Thomas*, Jesus stated, "Where the beginning is, there is also the ending." Indeed, this is so. Before the absolute nothingness called birth seemed to blind us, we knew what we were—and are. But this nothingness called birth did not, and could not, delete from us our full knowledge of the fact that we *are* the Christ that is God being Man. All the while, we have gone right on knowing this Absolute Truth. It has only seemed, for a little second of our eternal Being, that we dreamed otherwise. But now we *know* better.

Oh yes, we attentively read the statements of Absolute Truth, and we contemplate these Truths. We attentively listen to words of Absolute Truth, and we contemplate this Truth. However, we are contemplating the Truth, not the words we have been reading or hearing. The words only remind us of the fact that we already *know* these Truths. We joyously contemplate, reconsider, the Absolute Truth that our God, eternal Christ-Consciousness, has forever known, knows now, and will everlastingly know. Yes, *All is now, All is here, and we are That.*

Light and Love,
Marie S. Watts

February 1971

In the beginning was the Word, and the Word was with God, and the Word was God.

—John 1:1

Dear One,

Spring is definitely revealing all its freshness and Beauty here in Vista. The flowers are everywhere and in great masses of various colors. The hills are a riotous, gay variety of greens, intermingled with yellows, browns, and many colors that cannot be described. The green glossy leaves of the orange trees, with the bright oranges twinkling through the leaves, brings forth an, "Oh, isn't it wonderful!" We find ourselves laughing in sheer Joy at the Beauty of it all. No matter where we look, there is such Beauty, Beauty, *Beauty* that finally we find ourselves saying, "Oh, God, the All, how great is the Beauty that everyone and *everything is.* Thus, this is the Beauty that I am."

Yes, beloved One, you gaze upon all this Beauty, and you see the glory of *all* Substance, all Form. Then you see the Beauty *in*, and *as*, that which is beyond all Beauty, and suddenly there are no more words—only *Silence*, in the wondrous, boundless, limitless Beauty that is beyond all words. Thus it is.

There Are No "Tomorrows"

There are some words that are meaningful and others that are meaningless. The word *tomorrow* is meaningless. It is completely devoid of meaning because there is no Truth, or Fact, upon which it is based. Of course, this same fact is true of the word *yesterday*. There are no yesterdays. All—Everything, Everyone, all activity—exists only in the eternal Now. *Yesterday, today,* and *tomorrow* are words that refer to the same thing, and the fact itself is that *All is Now, Now is All.* Now is Eternity. Eternity is Now. Of course, this is only a way of saying there is no time.

Often we hear someone say, "Oh well, let's hope things will be better tomorrow." Things are never going to be better than they are right *Now.* How can God *become* All, when God *is* All? How can All *become* God, when All *is* God?

The word *imperfection* is a meaningless word. But if there were any such thing as imperfection, it would be eternal, omnipresent, infinite, and constant. Thus, there could never be an iota of Perfection anywhere. Absolute Perfection is an infinite, eternal, omnipresent Constant. It neither comes nor goes. It simply *is.* God *is* Absolute Perfection; thus, Absolute Perfection *is* God. God does not wait until tomorrow in order to *become* the Absolute Perfection that God *is* right now, constantly, infinitely, and eternally. God does not wait to become that which God is already, infinitely and eternally.

Beloved, the foregoing statements are power-filled statements of Absolute Truth. It would be well to contemplate these Absolute Truths and let your God-Self reveal whatever should be revealed in and as the Consciousness you are.

As we know all too well, the news media daily and hourly report their concept, or misconception, of a world in turmoil. Wars, atrocities, murders, dishonesty, intrigue, etc., are the feast the news media set before us each day. We do not ignore these claims to a presence and a power that is not God. Rather, we keep informed, as much as is necessary, as to the *apparent* situation in the world and specifically in our own beloved Nation.

You will recall that Moses had first to see his rod *apparently* become a serpent before he turned and faced it for what it seemed to be. But when Moses turned and actually faced the appearance called a serpent, he was able to perceive the faithful rod he had carried all the while. So we do not blind ourselves to the appearance of evil. Rather, we face it, we see it, and see right *through* its pretense; we see what it actually *is*, rather than what it *appears* to be.

It matters not whether the appearance of imperfection manifests itself as an imperfect world, nation, business, home, body, or whatever. It is all the same deception; it would *pretend* there is something that is not God, Absolute Perfection, present and active. In any seeming situation such as the foregoing, the necessity is always to face it squarely and actually see it as it *is*. Always the word *is* means *now*. It does not mean *tomorrow*. So we do not dawdle. Steadfastly, constantly, we continue to see Existence as it *is*.

Now, the question is often asked, "But how can I do this, when it seems so real?" Yes, it does—just at first— seem difficult, but it is not impossible. As always, we find the answers to this question in our beloved Bible:

> Judge not according to the appearance, but judge righteous judgment (John 7:24).

Yes, despite any appearance of imperfection, inharmony, treachery, etc., we are completely unmoved and unperturbed. We are not deceived. We just don't accept or believe there is *anything* other than God, and God being That. No matter how threatening the fallacious appearance may be, we just "Go forth and stand upon the mount before the Lord" (1 Kings 19:11). Yes, walk right up to it, face it, and "stand upon the mount," which means that we hold our attention, Consciousness, steadfastly and effortlessly at the very height of our seeing and Being. Oh, the winds may blow until it appears that surely we will be cast down upon the jagged rocks below. We may even seem to bend with the winds. But we *stand* and *stand* and *stand*!

Many there are who will sincerely try to convince us that we are mistaken, that indeed there is something terrible taking place. We do not try to change their sincere convictions. That is not within our province. Rather, we joyously stand at, and on, our mountain peak—Consciousness, God. Oh, it is a glorious experience, for there is no resistance and nothing to resist. We know the full and complete meaning of that beautiful statement found in Isaiah 26:3:

> Thou wilt keep him in perfect peace, whose mind
> is stayed on thee: because he trusteth in thee.

Yes, oh yes! We *know* the perfect peace because we know that perfect Peace is an Absolute Truth, God, ever-present and everywhere present infinitely, constantly, eternally, and *Now*. We have no trust, or faith, in anything but God, for there is nothing else or other than God. But most important of all is the sure knowledge that our Peace is the Peace which *is* this World, this planet Earth, Everything and Everyone that exists. We know there is no tomorrow in which this perfect Peace is going to come. We know that things will not be better or worse tomorrow, for *Now* is all there is. The forever Now *is* the Kingdom of Heaven, has forever been the Kingdom of Heaven, and will everlastingly be the glorious, immutable, joyous, perfect Kingdom of God. Behold, there is no other.

Light and Love,
Marie S. Watts

About the Author

During early childhood, Marie Watts began questioning: "Why am I? What am I? Where is God? What is God?"

After experiencing her first illumination at seven years of age, her hunger for the answers to these questions became intensified. Although she became a concert pianist, her search for the answers continued, leading her to study all religions, including those of the East.

Finally, ill and unsatisfied, she gave up her profession of music, discarded all books of ancient and modern religions, kept only the Bible, and went into virtual seclusion from the world for some eight years. It was out of the revelations and illuminations she experienced during those years, revelations that were sometimes the very opposite of what she had hitherto believed, that her own healing was realized.

During all the previous years, she had been active in helping others. After 1957, she devoted herself exclusively to the continuance of this healing work and to lecturing and teaching. Revelations continually came to her, and these have been set forth in this and every book.

To all seekers for Truth, for God, for an understanding of their own true Being, the words in her books will speak to your soul.

Made in the USA
Columbia, SC
08 November 2018